*This book is dedicated to my boys, Jack and Johnny.*
*May there always be wild rivers to quench your thirst*
*for exploration and discovery!*

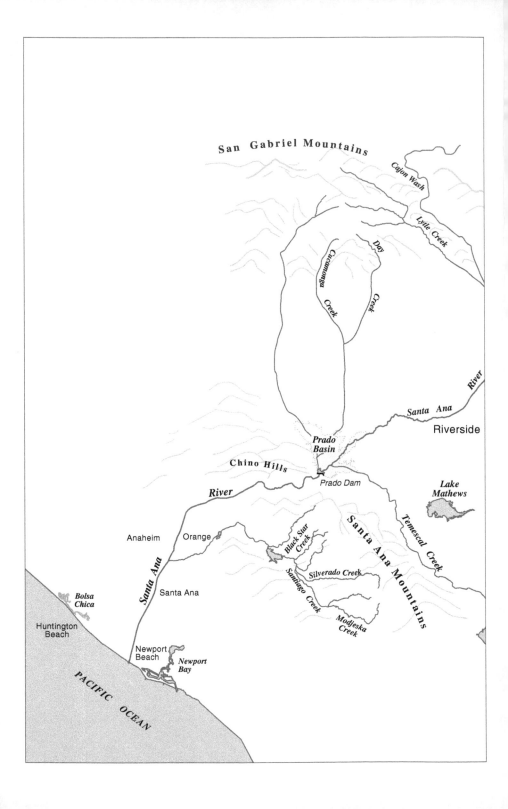

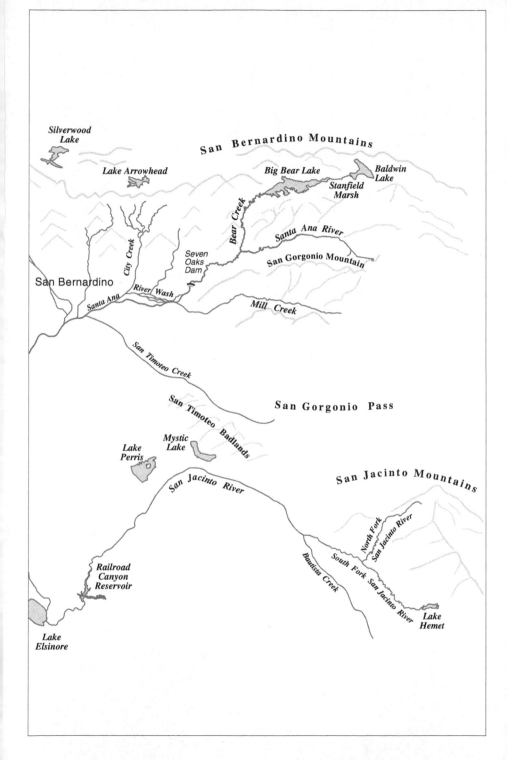

# SANTA ANA RIVER GUIDE

From Crest to Coast—
110 miles along
Southern California's
largest river
system

## PATRICK MITCHELL

 WILDERNESS PRESS

Santa Ana River Guide: From Crest to Coast—
110 miles along Southern California's largest river system

1st EDITION 2006

Copyright © 2006 by Patrick Mitchell

Front and back cover photos copyright © 2006 by Patrick Mitchell
Interior photos, except where noted, by Patrick Mitchell
Maps: Ben Pease
Book and cover design: Larry B. Van Dyke
Book editor: Eva Dienel

ISBN-13: 978-0-89997-411-8
ISBN-10: 0-89997-411-2

Manufactured in the United States of America

Published by: **Wilderness Press**
**PO Box 43673**
**Birmingham, AL 35243**
**(800) 443-7227; FAX (205) 326-1012**
**info@wildernesspress.com**
**www.wildernesspress.com**

Visit our website for a complete listing of our books
and for ordering information.

*Cover photo:*   The Santa Ana River in the San Bernardino Mountains *(inset)*
*Frontispiece:*   The Santa Ana River begins its journey in the San Bernardino
Mountains *(top)*, and flows into the Pacific Ocean *(bottom)*.

**SAFETY NOTICE:** Although Wilderness Press and the author have made every attempt to ensure that the information in this book is accurate at press time, they are not responsible for any loss, damage, injury, or inconvenience that may occur to anyone while using this book. You are responsible for your own safety and health. The fact that a trail is described in this book does not mean that it will be safe for you. Be aware that trail conditions can change from day to day. Always check local conditions and know your own limitations.

# CONTENTS

# SECTION II:
## GETTING TO, IN, AND ON THE RIVER   49

## Historical Sites and Cultural Resources   203

# ACKNOWLEDGMENTS

I would like to thank the many watershed advocates, educators, and wilderness defenders—from both nonprofits and government agencies (some of you are both)—who point people like me toward the river. All of the federal, state, county, and local park personnel and land managers who assisted me with this project deserve much credit. It is obvious that you shared with me the places you think are special, and your passion shows. I want to thank everyone at Wilderness Press for keeping this project on track. You are all professionals that make beginners like me look good. Thanks to the City of Santa Ana Parks, Recreation, and Community Services Agency for providing a work environment that encourages people to express and work with their passions. Thanks to Bobby Palmer for photos, and Matt Shook and Joel Robinson for photos and companionship on many SAR trips. Thanks to Dr. Brad Berger for his review and creative comments on the manuscript and his ability to help others think deeper. Most of all, I want to thank my family for putting up with my early-morning outings, weekends away, and countless hours in front of the computer, especially my wife, Shannon, for picking up everything I drop and still encouraging me to follow my dreams no matter how heavy my load gets. And thanks to the god that made rivers run through our lives.

# PREFACE

The Santa Ana River has always been a part of my life, even when I was not aware of it. In fact, this book rises from the ages-old experience of not knowing how important something is until it's gone. And unfortunately, the river I knew as a child is gone, at least to me.

Like most of the generation that grew up here in the 1970s, I took the river for granted at age 10 when I was busy catching tree frogs, fence lizards, and the occasional horned lizard along its banks. I believed these things would be there forever. The river was rich with critters, and it seemed that no matter how far I walked in a day, I would still find them. Every pool and puddle along the river had tadpoles in spring, and at night it was like a million individual frogs were singing to one another. It's no wonder these tiny amphibians earned the nickname "chorus frogs."

My friends and I would build whoop-di-dos and jumps for our BMX bikes in the countless acres of vacant land along the river's banks. Some kids in the neighborhood kept horses along the river and would ride up and down the waterway. We would ride skateboards in the smaller channels and pipes that fed the river. When youthful exuberance was more than we could control, the river provided miles of trails to run, ride, and explore, and we would do so until we ran out of sunlight or energy. Then we'd rest under the shady canopy of mature cottonwood trees and tell tall tales of past adventures.

When we were teenagers, the river provided an adult-free zone where bad words could be spoken without fear of repercussion. Here, we explored the wilderness of adolescence, as we experimented with the things our parents had warned us against. The river served as a corridor that seemed to connect to everywhere we needed to go. We used it to travel between each others' homes, thrift stores, and video arcades.

When I left Southern California in 1988 to attend college first in Santa Cruz and later in Prescott, Arizona, the Santa Ana River occupied only a small corner of my memory. But occasionally I was reminded of its importance to me. While swimming in the San Lorenzo River in the Santa Cruz Mountains, I imagined the Santa Ana River in centuries past, when natives and settlers enjoyed the river as a recreational destination. I later learned that the river was a vacation spot well into the 1950s. Fifth Street in Santa Ana was one of the most popular locations for a family to spend several days camped along its banks. Today, the river remains a place to escape the hot, dry summer days dished out in places like Pedley and Highlands.

In Arizona, I learned about riparian restoration and imagined a real forest along the banks of the Santa Ana—willows in place of concrete. Today, much of the Santa Ana River above Prado Dam is lined with willow and cottonwood forests, just like many rivers of the Southwest. I still imagine what the lower reaches through my old stomping grounds would be like if they were bordered by forest. I am routinely surprised by the pockets of wild nature that spring up where water rests or concrete cracks.

But even as I imagined a more natural Santa Ana River, another vision was being forged in the boardrooms of local governments and engineering firms. In 1986, the US Army Corps of Engineers and local flood-control agencies began working out final plans for the Santa Ana River Mainstem Project. At the time, the Corps of Engineers considered the Santa Ana River the most dangerous flood threat in the US, and it was this threat that finally convinced Congress to appropriate hundreds of millions of dollars toward improving the river's flood-conveyance capabilities. Their aim was to "fix" the river to a point that it could carry runoff from a rain event so big it is likely to occur only every 190 years. As a result of the project, the government built the Seven Oaks Dam at the foot of the San Bernardino Mountains, it reinforced the channels of two major river tributaries, and it covered much of the lower river in concrete. Although not complete at the time of this writing, Prado Dam is also being raised an additional 25 feet as part of the Mainstem Project.

By 1993, I had moved back to my childhood home, just a few blocks from the river in Garden Grove. Nonetheless, I was barely aware of how this massive project would change the river I loved, nor did I fully understand how the Santa Ana River had impacted my life. Instead, I was consumed with what I considered a more important effort—trying to stop the construction of a toll road through the San Joaquin Hills that made no economic sense and even less environmental sense. I thought saving that undeveloped area from destruction was a bigger priority than saving a river that ran through my older urban community.

I now consider this episode my greatest mistake as an environmental advocate. Not that the toll road should have been allowed—it was ultimately built anyway—but I now understand that the natural and human communities along the Santa Ana River also deserved someone to stand up in their defense. Unfortunately, the areas where I once roamed in search of small reptiles and amphibians, and in which I had my first wilderness experiences, have been, at least in part, covered by concrete. The river is now adorned with meaningless graffiti scrolled in a language spoken only by its author and a small, secret society of people who have learned the dialect.

When I rediscovered the Santa Ana as an adult, I mourned the loss of my childhood playground, and that encouraged me to further explore the river. I wondered if there was still a playground for the new youth along the river—a place for my children to run wild and discover why rivers have played such an important role in so many people's lives.

In 1999, I adopted Santiago Creek, the largest Orange County tributary to the river, as my home watershed. It still has a "soft" (unlined) bottom for nearly all of its length, and like the river itself, it is rich in culture and lore. I continue to work on this creek today, restoring habitat along its banks, leading tours, and often just sitting to listen to the stream's lessons of life.

Through my work on Santiago Creek and my own rediscovery of the river, I began to network with other groups and individuals working on, in, and along the river. It soon became apparent that there was a much larger movement growing in the watershed that wanted for the river what I did—better water quality, connectivity with more habitat, and recreational open space.

During this time, I discovered the Wildlands Conservancy, a Southern California-based nonprofit organization that operates on the mission of preserving natural open space and supporting programs that provide children with the opportunity to experience those places. I also heard about an important river meeting from Mike Wellborn, a fellow watershed advocate who worked for Orange County's watershed division. As it turned out, the meeting was held at the sheriff's office, and it provided me with the opportunity to meet others doing similar work. At this initial meeting, we discussed Santiago Creek and the potential to do environmental education along its banks. It was also the first meeting that led to the Santa Ana River Bike Program, which has, to date, given away nearly 1000 bikes to youth who complete a volunteer project related to the river and its environs.

In many ways, this book was borne out of that first meeting. It was a revelation to find that so many people were thinking of the river the way I was, and that some of them had been doing so since I was a kid. At the meeting, I met people from other areas along the river, including folks from Riverside and San Bernardino counties. I recognized what I had always suspected, that there was more to the river than the 15-mile stretch I had grown up with.

After that meeting, I began exploring the reaches upstream, and I studied the engineering plans and development proposals along the river. Ultimately, I found the playground I had been searching for, and I also found a new purpose: restoring the natural and recreational character of the Santa Ana River and its tributaries. I believe the best way to do this is to reconnect people with the river and to make the river the center of community life, which is also why I wrote this book.

Over the years, I have continued to explore the Santa Ana River—but not just at the river itself. I've explored its past in libraries and museums, and I have sought out and listened to the stories of old-timers who knew the river before I did. I rediscovered the Santa Ana River for myself and began to see how the river has always been a part of me—how it has influenced my life, my personal philosophies, and my actions.

My hope is that this book will help you, the reader, begin to see the river as I have, as a place where we can step away from our everyday stress and remember a calmer, more pure time when steelhead swam upstream, kids splashed in slow-moving water, and we all rested under the shade of mature cottonwoods. This book is one tiny step in my effort to restore the Santa Ana River to the prominence it deserves. I hope you join me!

# THE SANTA ANA RIVER:
## YESTERDAY
## AND TODAY

*left:* **The Big Bend, Santa Ana Canyon**

1

# INTRODUCTION

Beginning as a cold, crisp mountain stream in the high peaks of the San Bernardino Mountains, the Santa Ana River stretches for more than 110 miles, flowing through portions of San Bernardino, Riverside, and Orange counties and traversing boulder-strewn beds, deep canyons, concrete channels, and wetlands before finally reaching the Pacific Ocean at Huntington Beach. With a watershed that includes portions of the San Jacinto, San Gabriel, and Santa Ana mountains and encompasses more than 3000 square miles—a broad diversity of terrain, habitat, and cultural areas—the Santa Ana is the largest river system south of the Sierra Nevada mountains. It is also one of the most important rivers in Southern California.

## About This Book

Compiling information for this book was a gargantuan task. Not only was I charged with deciding how much of the watershed and which tributaries to cover, I also had to narrow down the number of recreation opportunities to include in the book. In the end, some of my selections were arbitrary, but I made most using a careful, methodical process.

Nonetheless, writing this book was a labor of love, and ultimately, I decided that the heart of this book should be the guide to the many parks, wilderness areas, nature centers, and historic sites of the Santa Ana River watershed. My emphasis on visiting the river is not because information about the natural and cultural history of the watershed is less important—in fact, it is more important than I first imagined. But experiencing the river first hand and seeing its natural resources is the

*left:* **Cold, clean, and fast: Santa Ana River in the high country**

3

best way to understand its natural history and learn how to protect the river.

When you see wild trout jump through cascading and frigid water of the upper river, or hear the song of least bells vireo in the disturbed landscape of the "Norco Burn," you develop an understanding of the river's importance. When you hike the steep road up Coal Canyon and see the circular tracks of a mature mountain lion heading toward Santa Ana Canyon and the 91 Freeway, you witness the importance of biological corridors that often follow rivers and streams in this watershed. When you jog or bike on the levy between the concrete walls of the lower river and the hundreds of homes that line it, you know that this is no place for a freeway. These are lessons you cannot learn from reading alone. They must be experienced.

Consider this book an experiential education on the natural history and conservation of the Santa Ana River. This book is a comprehensive guide to the Santa Ana River and much of its watershed, covering almost 100 parks, wilderness areas, nature centers, historic sites, and cultural attractions. It covers every major access point and many of the lesser-known ones, and fees, hours of operation, and future plans for each of the sites are included when available.

## How This Book Is Organized

This book begins with an introduction to the geography and natural and cultural history of the Santa Ana River. However, this is just an introduction; a full-length study of the river's ecology is warranted. The second section of this book is designed to provide all of the information necessary to plan a trip. More than 1 million acres of watershed can be explored from the access points, parks, and wilderness areas described here.

I have made an effort to focus on places that are free or available for a small fee. The many commercial operations along the river have been excluded, with the exception of equestrian facilities, which charge a fee either for boarding or renting horses. Equestrians have fewer places to ride as development gobbles up open space, and the river has a rich equine history. Golf courses, on the other hand, are not listed here because golfers have plenty of opportunities, which continue to multiply with increased development.

In order to ease the book's flow and comprehension, the river is divided into six reaches. These are not the reaches used by the Army Corps of Engineers or local flood-control agencies. Instead, I have chosen them based on certain characteristics unique to those areas and by landmarks such as mountains, dams, and freeways that define the reaches. These stretches of river share many characteristics, including vegetation type, wildlife populations, access points, trailheads, and trail lengths. In addition, the land-use patterns that border the river in each of these areas are similar throughout each reach.

As is common with rivers, some of the characteristics from upstream areas are carried downstream and may be common to more than one reach. In other words, the river pays no attention to the boundaries imposed by this guide, nor the boundaries of city, county, or state governments. Water follows the path of least resistance and carries with it whatever it must to reach its goal. This is simply a way of saying that similarities may be found in every reach of the river.

In some cases, there is very little open space along the river for long stretches, and access to the river may be restricted to support development up to its very edge. In these cases, where the river extends for some distance without a major access point, I describe the river and any trail, if one exists.

## The Six Reaches of the River

### Reach I: San Bernardino Mountains
Forty miles, from the river's headwaters at San Gorgonio Mountain and the Big Bear Valley down to the Seven Oaks Dam.

### Reach II: Santa Ana River Wash and Upper Inland Empire
Twenty miles, from Seven Oaks Dam downstream to Hwy. 60 at Riverside.

### Reach III: Santa Ana River Regional Park and Lower Inland Empire
Twenty-three miles, from Hwy. 60 to Prado Dam.

### Reach IV: Santa Ana Canyon
Fouteen miles, from Prado Dam to the 91 Freeway crossing.

### Reach V: Orange County Coastal Plain
Fifteen miles, from 91 Freeway to the 405 Freeway.

### Reach VI: Orange Coast and the River Mouth
Five miles, from 405 freeway to the ocean, including historic outlets along the coast.

Following the sections on the six reaches of the river, this book covers destinations along four of the river's main tributaries: Mill Creek, Lytle Creek, San Jacinto River, and Santiago Creek. These tributaries are described in order, beginning in the upper watershed and following the watershed downstream. Finally, the book includes a section on historical and cultural resources. The Santa Ana is the oldest river in Southern California, and it is rich with history. This section introduces you to the historical resources that are close to the river and offer easy access.

## How to Use This Book

The destinations in this book range from wilderness and roadless areas to small urban pocket parks, and depending on where you go, you may be able to hike, walk a nature trail, learn about natural or cultural history at a visitor center, enjoy a picnic at an urban park, or simply walk down to the riverside to enjoy the solitude.

| Map Legend | | | |
|---|---|---|---|
| Featured Trail | - - - - - - - - | Major River | ———— |
| Other Trail | - - - - - - - - - | Major Stream | ———— |
| Road | ▬▬▬▬ | Major Flood-Control Channel | ———— |
| Freeway | ════ | | |
| Graded Road | - - - - | Body of Water | ⬭ |
| Point of Interest | **1** | Marsh/Swamp | ⸳⸳⸳ |
| Picnic Area | 🛆 | Dam and Reservoir | |
| Camping Area | 🛆 | | |
| Peak | ▲ | Dam and Flood Zone | |
| Gate | •—• | Wash | |
| Building | ▬ | | |
| Railroad | ·—·—·—· | Park or Preserve | |
| County Line | — — — | | |
| North Arrow | 🧭 | National Forest | |
| | | Wilderness Area | |

## Santa Ana River Crest to Coast Trails

The Santa Ana River is home to one of the Southland's longest trail systems, the Santa Ana River Crest to Coast Riding and Hiking Trail and Bikeway. When complete, this 100-mile trail will stretch from the northern toe of San Gorgonio Mountain to the river's mouth at the border between Huntington and Newport beaches. Designated a National Recreation Trail in 1977, the system actually includes two trails—one paved pathway, the Santa Ana River Bikeway, for cycling, and an unpaved path, the Santa Ana River Trail, for hiking, horse riding, and mountain biking.

The hiking/equestrian trail includes just a few short stretches that are yet to be complete, but it is possible to ride or walk the entire way. As recently as the 1990s, equestrians rode the entire length, camping at several locations along its path. Walkers often tread along the lower stretches, and mountain bikers love the single-track stretch that connects Morton Peak with Hwy. 38 above Barton Flats. Hikers in the mountain stretch can access numerous other trails, including the Pacific Crest Trail, and routes into the San Gorgonio Wilderness.

At the time of this writing, the bike trail was a total of nearly 70 miles, with an expected completion date sometime in 2008. The 25-mile Orange County stretch is complete, but one of the major gaps at the time of this writing was at Prado Dam where Orange, San Bernardino, and Riverside counties meet. Another gap was just above Prado Basin and a few short stretches still needed work through Santa Ana River Regional Park. The San Bernardino section of the trail is popular with commuters because it connects to many county offices and downtown business. At the time of this writing, the last major gap to be filled there was the river wash area at the foot of the San Bernardino Mountains.

When the hiking/equestrian and bike routes are complete, this trail system will connect the urban and rural communities of three counties and 17 cities with the wilderness of two national forests and hundreds of thousands of acres of open space. It's possible to access both of these trails in many of the trips in this book.

This book is designed to provide all of the information necessary to plan a trip to the river. As such, each trip includes highlights, trip location and river access points, season and hours of operation, facilities available, contact information, and information about camping and permits (where required). Access points for the Santa Ana River Crest to Coast Trails also are provided, and each trip description offers a variety of activities, from hiking to picnicking to learning about the cultural and natural history of the river.

There are also several maps included throughout the book to show you where to find each of the trips and where the reaches and tributaries are located. The legend on page 6 provides a key to the features in the maps.

## A Final Note

As you begin to explore the river, you'll discover that the trails, natural resources, and recreational areas are dynamic. There are trail repairs being made, trees being planted, and parks being refurbished. In places where there were only urban lots, now there are patches of habitat or interpretive signs.

Many times, these project are being carried out by nonprofit organizations, friends groups, and community volunteers. Sometimes the projects are carried out by cities, counties, or other land managers, and sometimes there is an elected official in the driver's seat. But even when there is a mayor, supervisor, or governor leading the charge, there is usually a concerned and passionate citizen or community group pushing them to the front.

In order to increase your ability to fully participate in the river and its renaissance, this book includes a resource guide (page 235) to the nonprofit and government agencies that have connections to the river. To further illustrate these connections, the stories of some of these groups and individuals are also provided, as is a discussion of current and future threats to the Santa Ana River and its watershed (page 221). Finally, you will find information on how to get involved in the effort to preserve and restore the Santa Ana River.

So take this book and read it. Use it as a guide to get on the river and to understand its mechanics and its resources. Visit the described sites and explore the wild places the river leads you to.

# GEOGRAPHY OF THE SANTA ANA RIVER

The Santa Ana River drains approximately 3200 square miles of Southern California, receives water from four distinct mountain ranges that together are as high as the Himalaya, and flows past more than one third of California's population. Like all great rivers, the Santa Ana has tributaries that, like fingers connecting to the palm, bring water to the main stem of the river. The mountains, valleys, and tributaries of the river are reviewed here as the sun sees them—from east to west—beginning with the San Jacinto Mountains and working west to the Santa Ana Mountains, and, finally, to the coastal plain and mouth of the river at the Pacific Ocean.

The San Jacinto Mountains rise to more than 10,000 feet and constitute the final wall, preventing the coast and its cooling influences from reaching the desert. These mountains drain westward into the San Jacinto River, which is the southern and easternmost tributary to the Santa Ana River. The San Jacinto River feeds Lake Elsinore, which then drains into Temescal Wash, which joins the Santa Ana River in the Prado Basin. Interstate 10 crosses the pass that separates the San Jacinto Mountains from the San Bernardino Mountains. The range is easily accessed from State Route 243 off Interstate 10 between Palm Springs and Banning. State Route 74 crosses the San Jacinto range.

Elsinore Valley is in the rain shadow of the Santa Ana Mountains, but it contains a large natural lake. Lake Elsinore is California's largest "sag pond"—a lake that formed on top of a fault line due to earthquake activity that allowed underground water to rise to the surface. Today, the lake is fed by the San Jacinto River and is often used by the

Lake Elsinore is a big sag pond separating San Jacinto River from Temescal Creek.

Metropolitan Water District to store imported water from the Colorado River. Lake Elsinore is a popular recreational lake for boating and fishing and an excellent bird-watching site.

State Route 74 roughly follows the San Jacinto River out of the San Jacinto Mountains to Lake Elsinore and then up over the Santa Ana Mountains to Mission San Juan Capistrano and the ocean. From the lake, Temescal Wash follows Interstate 15 north to the city of Corona and the 91 Freeway, where it drains into the Santa Ana River.

The San Bernardino Mountains, including 11,502-foot San Gorgonio Mountain, are the highest mountains in Southern California. The Santa Ana River proper begins just north of San Gorgonio Mountain. Fed by snowmelt and springs, the river here is more like a stream, 10 feet wide and fast moving. This stretch of river is an angler's paradise, well known for its prize trout. Bear Creek, Mill Creek, and San Timoteo Wash are among the major tributary streams that drain the San Bernardino Mountains. Baldwin and Big Bear lakes are also within the Santa Ana River watershed in the San Bernardino Mountains. Primary access to the river's headwaters and peaks of the San Gorgonio Wilderness is from State Hwy. 38, however, highways 18 and 330 also lead into the San Bernardino National Forest. Interstate 15 crosses the western terminus of the range at Cajon Pass. This book's journey begins high in the San Bernardino Mountains.

The San Gabriel Mountains rise to the west of, but in line with, the San Bernardino Mountains. Separated by the San Andreas fault at the Cajon Pass (Interstate 15), these mountains provide the snowy backdrop most Southern Californians enjoy on clear winter days. Mt. Baldy sits atop the crest of this range, at an elevation of 10,080 feet above sea level. Cajon Wash and Lytle Creek are major tributaries draining the San Gabriel Mountains and feeding into the Santa Ana River. The San Gabriel and Los Angeles rivers also drain the San Gabriel Mountains. The best access to this range is from state highways 138 and 2. Interstate 15 crosses the northern terminus of the San Gabriels at Cajon Pass.

The Inland Empire is made up of numerous cities within Riverside and San Bernardino counties. For the most part, the river here has been left natural, although not always pristine. It is a popular destination for the bustling communities of Riverside, Colton, and San Bernardino. There have been only minimal flood-control efforts on this stretch of river, however, some of the tributaries have been "improved" to support new, large-scale development. The Inland Empire is one of the fastest-growing communities in the US, and the area is crossed by interstates 10, 15, and 215, as well as state routes 71, 91, 60, and many surface roads.

Chino Basin is a large, relatively flat agricultural area. In fact, the basin's dairy cattle population outnumbers people 2-to-1. The basin is a low-lying valley surrounded by mountains and hills, which form a bottleneck where the Santa Ana River squeezes between the Chino Hills and Santa Ana Mountains. Prado Dam was constructed at this bottleneck in 1941 to protect downstream areas from flooding. The wetlands and riparian forests behind the dam are today some of the most important habitats in Southern California, with more than 4000 acres of willow-cottonwood forest and other riparian and wetland communities. Chino Basin is bounded by State Route 71 on the western edge at the foot of the Chino Hills, State Route 91 on the south, State Route 60 to the north, and Interstate 15 on the east.

The Santa Ana Mountains comprise the westernmost range in the watershed and they are only a little more than half the height of the other ranges found here. Santiago Peak, the highest in the range at 5840 feet, is the headwaters for Santiago Creek, the largest tributary in the watershed. Irvine Lake is fed by Santiago Creek and is a popular fishing location. Santiago Creek then flows through the cities of Orange and Santa Ana, where it meets the Santa Ana River. Hwy 74 is the only highway that crosses the range, however, attempts to build additional roads over the Santa Anas come up regularly. Santiago Canyon Road and the 241 Toll Road wind along the western slope of the range. Interstate 15 follows the eastern foot of the mountains, and State Route 91 meets the northern foot of the Santa Ana Mountains at the Santa Ana River.

The "coastal plain" is the name commonly given to the gently sloping area west of the Santa Ana Mountains between the Chino/Whittier Hills at the north and the San Joaquin Hills to the south. This is also the area Juan Gaspar de Portola named the Valley of Saint Anne (Santa Ana Valley) in 1769. Today, the river is confined to a channel as it flows across the plain, but, historically, the river here was often very wide and multi-channeled. From Prado Dam to the city of Santa Ana border, the river is soft bottom, but in many locations it has concrete or riprap walls. This area is managed as a groundwater recharge area. After entering the city of Santa Ana, the river is confined to a concrete channel for the next 7 miles of its route to the ocean. Interstate 5 and state routes 22, 55, 57, and 405 all contact the river here, as do numerous surface streets. El Camino Real crosses the Santa Ana River in this area, where the river, Interstate 5, and Chapman Ave. all come together.

The Santa Ana River mouth is a small estuary forming the boundary between Newport and Huntington beaches. Known to local surfers as the river jetties, this area is a popular beach in summer and popular with bird-watchers throughout the year. Because the river is confined to a channel, it is almost completely separated from the numerous marshes that line the coast in this area. Historically, however, the river fed the rich marshlands along the coast and inland up to the Santa Ana and Garden Grove areas.

Prior to the 1920s, the river was a dynamic system, often flowing in several braided channels and feeding extensive freshwater, brackish, and saltwater marshes reaching more than 10 miles inland. In fact, the river moved across the coastal plain and emptied into the ocean at three different locations over the last century and a half. Newport Bay and the Bolsa Chica Wetlands are both historic outlets of the Santa Ana River and are included here as part of the river watershed. The river's mouth and its historic outlets and estuaries can be accessed from the Pacific Coast Hwy., State Route 1.

# NATURAL HISTORY OF THE SANTA ANA RIVER

Natural history is a general term that refers to the study of nature, or plants, animals, and other elements and how they all relate to one another. Unlike ecology, natural history is not experimental and includes geology, meteorology, and other natural phenomena. In short, it is the observational study of landscapes.

The Santa Ana River flows through one of the most important landscapes on the planet. The renowned naturalist E.O. Wilson has described the Southern California Floristic Province, through which the Santa Ana River flows, as one of about 10 biological "hot spots" in the world. Many plants and animals here are found nowhere else in the world. Some of them are on the verge of extinction, while others are as ubiquitous as the common housefly.

This chapter is an introduction to the natural history of the Santa Ana River, its geology, vegetation communities, and wildlife—including endangered species—and how they relate to each other. This is only an introduction, however. The natural history of the Santa Ana River is worthy of its own full-length book.

The Santa Ana River watershed is home to hundreds of species of wildlife—at least 200 species of birds, 50 mammals, 13 reptiles, 7 amphibians, and 15 fish. More than a dozen species are protected by state and federal endangered species laws, and more deserve protection.

The unique combination of climate, topography, and geology make the watershed a special place. The river and its tributaries originate above treeline in alpine meadows and flow through conifer forests, chaparral, and into the desert, and then over coastal passes, through

13

sage scrub, cities, and, finally, out to sea. Quality riparian forests line much of the water's route. In fact, waters of the Santa Ana River cross every life zone in California.

The climate of the watershed is just as diverse as the landscape. At its headwaters, the river is cold and the earth is frozen for part of the year. Winters bring heavy snows and temperatures often dip well below freezing where the river begins. Rarely does it snow in the lower watershed, but it does rain an average of 10 to 12 inches a year.

Spring is, of course, the season of rebirth, and during this time, the watershed thaws to life. The hillsides turn green and hundreds of wildflower species add a splash of color to the landscape. Cottonwoods, willows, and sycamores grow new leaves, and the melting snow travels toward the ocean under shaded forests that John Muir called ribbons of "tropical luxuriance."

Summers in the mountains are short and thunderstorms occur throughout the season. This is still, however, the best time to explore the wild canyons and tributaries of the upper Santa Ana River. At higher elevations, the flowers bloom late and insects are at a minimum. The explorer has unlimited access to deep forests and high peaks. However, temperatures often top 100°F between Seven Oaks Dam and Prado Dam during the summer. Below Santa Ana Canyon, the coastal influence is strong, and the summer temperature is often 10 degrees cooler here than it is above Prado Dam.

Autumn is a time of change in the watershed. Colors turn from emerald green to golden brown and yellow. The cottonwoods, willows, sycamores, and alders begin to drop their leaves, the nights become cold, and the river's flow decreases as the land prepares to take a long winter's nap.

Whatever the season, the Santa Ana River offers the naturalist plenty to see, study, and contemplate.

# GEOLOGY
# OF THE SANTA ANA
# RIVER

In Southern California, dirt is primarily decomposed rock, and sometimes that decomposed rock is in its second or third life, having once been part of a mountain that was eroded, recompressed into sandstone, and then broken down again. In the Santa Ana River watershed, there are dozens of kinds of rocks from each of the three rock types—sedimentary, igneous, and metamorphic. These rocks represent the earliest history in the Santa Ana River watershed.

The Santa Ana River, however, is older than many of the mountains it drains, having cut a path or canyon as those mountains grew. In particular, this is the case with the Santa Ana Mountains and Chino Hills along the Elsinore-Whittier fault. The river is the oldest in Southern California and has witnessed many mountain ranges grow taller over eons of time.

The Santa Ana River drains more than 3000 square miles of the Peninsular and Transverse ranges of Southern California, which are referred to as Cismontane Southern California or "the ocean side of the mountains." The Transverse Ranges are those Southern California mountains with ridgelines running along an east-west axis and separating Los Angeles from Bakersfield and the rest of the Central Valley. The Peninsular Ranges, including the Los Angeles Basin, run north-south and separate the basin from Palm Springs and the Colorado Desert. All of these mountains are "fault-block" mountains, meaning that they grew from earthquakes. Together, these mountains form the lip of the bowl that is the Los Angeles Basin. Three rivers drain into this bowl and empty into the Pacific Ocean: the Los Angeles, San Gabriel, and Santa Ana rivers.

Three major fault zones with hundreds of smaller individual faults dot the area. The most famous of these is, of course, the San Andreas fault, which is responsible for uplifting the San Bernardino and San Gabriel mountains of the Transverse Ranges. The other two fault zones are responsible for the Peninsular Ranges. The San Jacinto fault is the mother of the San Jacinto and Santa Rosa mountains, while the Elsinore-Whittier fault has raised the Santa Ana Mountains and Chino Hills.

The only dams on the Santa Ana River are actually constructed on top of major faults. The larger of the two, Seven Oaks Dam, is constructed on top of the San Andreas fault, while the Prado Dam is on top of the Whittier-Ellsinore fault.

Because the mountains of this region have grown as one large piece of earth rams against another, many layers of rock are exposed, as the latter piece is folded and pushed up. These layers can be seen in the river and stream canyons that finger out of the mountains. The steep and rugged canyons are common among young mountains like those of the Santa Ana River watershed because the forces of nature have not yet worn them down and smoothed their edges. Instead, the history of the area is displayed in layers, like a vertical timeline. The exposed earth makes the watershed a delight for the amateur as well as the expert geologist.

The headwaters of the Santa Ana River are the high points of each of the mountain ranges. San Gorgonio Mountain, in the San Bernardino Mountains, is the highest, at 11,502 feet. In the San Gabriels, 10,080-foot Mt. Baldy is the highest. San Jacinto Peak, the highest of the Peninsular Ranges, is 10,805 feet. The Santa Ana Mountains are half the height of the others, with Santiago Peak reaching only 5840 feet.

The rock found in the San Gabriel and San Bernardino mountains is the oldest in California. Because of the arid climate of this region and the relative lack of glaciation, there has been less erosion than in northern ranges, leaving the oldest rocks to cap our local mountains. Some of the rock found here is more than 1.7 billion years old. These metamorphic rocks are of gneiss and schist, and they are often dark gray or black, with tints of green. Included among these are the San Gabriel Anorthosite, Mendenhall Gneiss, and, the oldest of all, Augen Gneiss. Road cuts in the high reaches of the ranges are the best places to find these rocks.

**San Gorgonio Mountain is a four-season wilderness playground.**

The very old rocks mentioned earlier rest on top of the Southern California Batholith, which means "deep rock." The gabbros and granites of the Southern California Batholith are igneous in nature and formed as molten magma cooled deep beneath the surface between 75 million and 100 million years ago. This granite represents the core of all of our local mountains.

Much of the area drained by the Santa Ana River is made up of sedimentary rock, which, in the lower watershed, can reach depths of nearly 20,000 feet. This relatively new rock was created as sediment laid down by wind, rivers, and streams or in vast shallow seas was heated and compacted over time. Most of the sedimentary rock in the watershed is between 12 million and 25 million years old and originated in the Miocene Epoch. These distinct layers of stone, or strata, are often red or yellow in color and have obvious contrasting layers.

There are numerous places in the watershed to explore the geologic features and characteristics of the Santa Ana River's rocks and soil. Follow any stream, road, or trail in the hills and mountains of the Santa Ana River watershed, and you'll be sure to see some of the unique formations and characteristics of its geologic history.

Cajon Pass separates the San Bernardino and San Gabriel mountains via the San Andreas fault. This is the greatest of all faults in the region and is a geology explorer's dream. As the earth has bumped, rubbed, and folded, numerous layers of rock have been upturned. This location exposes sedimentary, as well as metamorphic and granitic layers.

Although no comparison to the likes of Yosemite Valley, the north slope of San Gorgonio Mountain was home to the southernmost glaciers in North America. The boulder-strewn cirque of the San Gorgonio Glacier has been dated at somewhere between 5000 and 25,000 years old. Early-season hikes on the mountain, when snow still covers the valley, provide a glimpse of what the area looked like during the last ice age when ice and nearly permanent snow covered the area.

The deep and steep canyon of Mill Creek is another good place to view some of the watershed's geologic story. Here, potato sandstone is visible on steep, stream-cut cliffs and road cuts. The soft, geometric layers appear like lasagna, with alternating beige, brown, and gray.

The Gavilan Hills are also unique geologic sites in the watershed, though somewhat distant from the river itself. The hills form a plateau between the Santa Ana River and its tributary, the San Jacinto River. Many large boulders dot the area and are somewhat of a commodity, often sold by local landowners to those who use them as landscape features. Several vernal pools, rare geologic and biologic features, are located in this area.

Gold, however, is what put the Gavilan Hills on the map. It is believed that as early as 1820, gold was being mined in the area. More than $2 million worth of gold was taken out of the Good Hope Mine over about a 90-year span. Some old-timers claim that "there's more gold to be got," but it can't be a lot because nobody is working very hard to get it. The Good Hope Mine has been closed for more than three decades.

Gold also was discovered in the upper watershed in Holcomb and Bear valleys in 1860. This gold rush brought thousands of people to the mountains, where they established towns, logging operations, and more. Gold is still mined in the Holcomb Valley, and some say the main vein has yet to be found; others hope it never is.

Farther down the watershed, the sediments stripped from the mountains are deposited by the river and bleached by the sun, creating a white, permeable sand. This sand contributes to the Delhi Sand Dunes, the largest remaining dune system in the South Coast Bioregion. The nature and location of these sands often puts them in the way of development, and the bulldozers usually win. The Delhi sands flower loving fly lives only in the soft sands of the Santa Ana River watershed and has become increasingly rare as these sand dunes decrease. The sandy habitat exists between Colton and the Prado Dam.

## Delhi Sands Flower Loving Fly

**STATUS:** Federally endangered

**DESCRIPTION:** Adult flies are 1 inch long and generally gray-brown with dark brown spots and large, bright green eyes. The Delhi sands flower loving flies *(Rhaphiomidas terminatus adominalis)* are agile fliers sometimes compared to humming birds because of their hovering ability. The flies are known to feed on California buckwheat *(Eriogonum fasciculatum)* but may also feed on other local native plants.

**LIFE CYCLE:** Adult flies reproduce in August and September. Females lay up to 50 eggs and likely choose locations based on preferred vegetation associations. Larval stage live just beneath surface of the soil for as long as two years. Little is known about the pupae stage. Adults then emerge to feed on nectar of native plants.

**HABITAT:** Found in the Delhi sands soil series of Riverside and San Bernardino counties. The Delhi series once covered more than 40 square miles, but less than 3 percent remains today. Most of the remaining habitat is in the Colton, Jurupa Hills, Prado, and Fontana areas. The vegetation association found in this soil type is a sand-dune-associated community that contains California buckwheat, sand verbena, and other native plants.

**CONSERVATION:** The remaining Delhi sands habitat is in rapidly developing areas, and even when protected, the habitat is threatened by increased human interactions. These activities include residential and commercial development, off-road vehicles, and collecting. Some of the habitat for the Delhi sands flower loving fly is included in the Western Riverside Multi-Species Habitat Conservation Plan and other habitat conservation agreements. However, any hope of recovery is contingent on preserving and restoring all of the remaining habitat.

Santiago Creek is the largest tributary in the lower watershed, and one of the finest places to explore the colorful strata laid down under vast shallow seas. The red rocks region below Blackstar Canyon is part of the Sespe Formation and is an attractive cliff with varying hues of iron red and cinnabar forming distinct strata. Above the red rocks area in Silverado Canyon, fossil hunters have found sharks' teeth, fossilized redwood, and even a pladosuarus, a duck-billed dinosaur. Many small shell fossils have been found in the limestone boulders that wash down the creek, making an expedition to any reach of Santiago Creek a geology explorer's dream.

In 1877, silver and coal were discovered in the canyons of the Santa Ana Mountains, creating boomtowns that rivaled any in the Wild West. Coal actually was discovered a decade earlier, but there was no demand for it at the time. Once the railroads reached the town of Santa Ana in 1878, more than 100 wagonloads of coal were hauled there weekly. By 1887, both the coal and silver booms had ended.

Early explorers of the Santa Ana River watershed described the use of tar by the indigenous people of the region. They coated everything from baskets to boats with the gooey petroleum to improve their buoyancy and water-carrying capacity. In the 1900s, that tar led speculators to drill for oil. Some were successful and much of the Santa Ana River watershed from Huntington Beach to the Chino Hills was tapped for its petroleum reserves. Today, only a few of the more than 10,000 wells that were drilled still produce oil. Most of those are located on the edge of Chino Hills State Park and along the Huntington Beach coast near the Bolsa Chica Wetlands.

At least as important and probably more valuable is the water that lies beneath the Santa Ana River. In the river's infancy, it was a larger and more powerful river, with the ability to move huge amounts of rock and soil. It first carved a deep basin in what is now the coastal plain of Orange County and dumped the debris in the Pacific Ocean, creating the shoreline we know today. The river then began to break down the San Gabriel and San Bernardino mountains, depositing the sand, gravel, and sediment into the deep coastal basin.

For millennia, the Santa Ana River has been filling that basin with trillions of gallons of water. A fraction of that water is available to us through wells and an elaborate delivery system. In fact, more than half of the water used in Orange County is pumped from the Santa Ana River aquifer. Today, this groundwater basin is considered the most active on the planet, meaning more water is put in and taken out of here than at any other aquifer in the world.

# FLORA AND FAUNA OF THE SANTA ANA RIVER

Scientists always have tried to classify and connect or group organisms as a way to better study and understand them. Biotic Zonation is the classification of landscapes based on elevation, slope, aspect, dominant vegetation type, geographic locale, and other natural characteristics. There are numerous schools of biotic classification, however, and I rely primarily on the California Plant Community classifications for this book. This system uses dominant vegetation to classify each community.

The Santa Ana River flows through nearly every vegetation community found in the region. The river serves as a corridor for the movement of plants and animals and is likely the reason many of the desert plants occur close to the coast. For example, the only naturally occurring Great Basin sagebrush in Orange County grows along the Santa Ana River in Santa Ana Canyon, but the plant is common in the higher elevations of the watershed. The theory is that seeds were carried downstream by the river, or blown in by Santa Ana Winds, which follow the river's path.

The next few pages provide brief descriptions of the vegetation communities crossed by the Santa Ana River and some of the wildlife that might be encountered in those communities.

## Alpine

The high peaks of the San Jacinto and San Bernardino mountains are home to the alpine community of Southern California. Occurring at the headwaters of the river above 10,500 feet in the San Bernardinos, this land above the trees is home to extreme conditions including intensely cold, harsh winds, extended sun exposure, and shallow soil conditions. At a first and distant glance, much of the alpine zone appears to be solid rock, however, with closer inspection it's evident that a rich and hardy collection of plants and animals survives in this community. Among them are sedges, paintbrushes, and various phlox species.

Few wildlife species are spotted at this high elevation. Among the species here are black bears; though they rarely go above 10,000 feet in the San Bernardinos, they have been spotted near the peak of San Gorgonio. Mostly small mammals such as mice and chipmunks are found in this area.

## Subalpine

The subalpine forest is the community below the alpine zone and is the highest forest community, at elevations between 9500 and 11,000 feet. This forest, however, is often sparse, with trees bunched up in areas protected from the elements. Indeed, conditions here are still quite harsh, with strong winds, extreme temperatures, and extended periods of frost.

Soil in the subalpine community tends to be deeper than that of the alpine zone, which allows the establishment of trees. These trees, however, tend to be gnarled, twisted, and stunted due to the intensity of the conditions in which they grow. Most of the trees in this community are five-needle pines that, although small in stature, often grow to be quite old. Some limber pines in the Santa Ana watershed are more than 2000 years old. Junipers are also found in this community, and they differ from the pines by having scale-like leaves rather than needles. Chinquapin bushes are common in areas where water is mostly absent or the soil is rocky and the forest open. The fruit of these shrubs resembles chestnuts.

Mountain chickadees and other birds can be heard in the trees of this community, but they are sometimes difficult to see. More common, or at least more noticeable, is the Clark's nutcracker. This black and gray, jay-sized bird collects seeds such as acorns and pine nuts and buries them in shallow caches in the high-country soil with the hope of finding them later when food is more scarce. Occasionally, these seeds sprout, and the nutcracker has been credited with many reforestation efforts. Chipmunks, ground squirrels, and even the occasional mule deer will be found in this community.

## Lodgepole Forest

The lodgepole forest ranges in elevation from 8000 to 10,500 feet and is named for the tall, straight trees used by the native tribes of the Great Plains for tepee building. This forest can vary in appearance depending on the exposure of the trees. In areas where the trees are blasted by wind, they are short and often twisted; in protected areas, the trees grow close together and straight up. One of the largest lodgepole pines in the state grows near Big Bear Lake. That tree reaches more than 110 feet high and its trunk measures nearly 7 feet in diameter.

Wildlife is common in this community. Chipmunks, ground squirrels, and other small mammals frequently are seen darting in and out of shrubs and forest duff. In particular, the golden-mantled ground squirrel is regularly spotted along trails in the zone.

## Yellow Pine Forest

Below the lodgepole forest is the yellow pine forest, which occurs between 5000 and 9500 feet in the Santa Ana watershed. Like all of the forest communities, it is higher in the San Bernardino Mountains than it is in the San Jacinto or San Gabriel ranges. The yellow pine forest covers the most area of the mountain vegetation communities, except, perhaps, for chaparral.

Dominated by Jeffrey pine, this community is one of the most recognizable forest types because it is the community in which many old westerns were made, including the classic television series *Bonanza*. Ponderosa pine and black oaks are common in this community, and small willow trees and shrubs follow watercourses, standing out from the taller trees that grow above the stream banks.

This is the most common community in the mountains for deer, black bear, and long-tailed weasels. Birds include many migratory warblers, nuthatches, and woodpeckers. The western gray squirrel also is common in the trees here.

## Upper Chaparral

Between elevations of 4000 and 6500 feet, we find the upper chaparral community. Dominated by manzanitas and mountain mahogany, this community is always dense and difficult to navigate. Once, while exploring the Santa Ana Mountains just below Santiago Peak, I found it easiest to move through the mature upper chaparral by getting down on all fours and crawling under it.

Like its lower cousin, this evergreen community is known for its sclerophyllous leaves. These tough, leathery leaves help the plant conserve water during high temperatures, strong winds, and extended seasonal droughts. On north-facing slopes, one may also encounter big cone Douglas fir and coulter pines within the upper chaparral community.

Although black bears tend to avoid this community, this once was the historic haunt of the California grizzly, which has been extinct since the early 1900s. Mountain lions, coyotes, and badgers all live here.

## Mountain Lion

**STATUS:** The mountain lion is protected from hunting throughout California. The population of lions that lives in the Santa Ana Mountains and crosses the Santa Ana River to get to the Chino Hills is in serious decline due to isolation from other populations. Mountain lions could be encountered almost anywhere in the watershed from the headwaters to Santa Ana Canyon.

**DESCRIPTION:** Mountain lions (*Felis concolor*), also called cougars, pumas, and panthers, are the largest predators in the Santa Ana River watershed. An adult lion can weigh as much as 200 pounds, though most males are around 150 pounds and females are about 110 pounds. Lions are generally golden brown with patches of white on their face and underside. Their distinctive long tails are usually darker at the tip. Mountain lions will eat almost any small animal, including deer, rabbits, raccoons, and birds.

**LIFE CYCLE:** Mountain lions are solitary animals, maintaining individual ranges of 100 square miles or more. Ranges will overlap with those of the opposite sex but rarely with those of the same sex. Female lions will give birth to up to four kittens, which stay with their mother for 18 months, after which time they disperse to claim their own territory. It is at this time that many lion-human encounters occur. Lions live 10 to 12 years on average but have survived in captivity for more than 20 years.

**HABITAT:** Mountain lions can be found throughout the western US and parts of the East, though they are mostly absent from the Midwest and plains states. In the Santa Ana River watershed, lions could be

## Lower Chaparral

Lower chaparral, one of the most common communities in California, is found at elevations of 1000 to 5000 feet and consists of plants with smaller sclerophylous leaves, including California lilacs and chamise on drier, south-facing slopes. On the north side, scrub oaks and redberry or holly-leaf cherry dominate the community.

Many reptiles are found in this community. Rattlesnakes, mountain king snakes, horned lizards, and others could be encountered when traveling through this vegetation zone. Remember that rattlesnakes live along most of the Santa Ana River; if you encounter one, stop, move

encountered in the forests of the San Bernardino Mountains down to the alluvial scrub of the river wash area, however, they rarely will be seen in areas without dense cover. Though it is possible that lions may come down as far as the Santa Ana River Regional Park, it is not likely that any regularly visit this area. Mountain lions do cross the river at Coal Canyon as they move back and forth between the Santa Ana Mountains and the Chino Hills. It is likely that these same lions visit the Prado Basin on occasion.

**CONSERVATION:** Mountain lions inhabit almost every natural community in the watershed and in many places are more common than people think. However, this wide-ranging mammal requires more than just a large island of open space. Each of their home ranges must connect to the home range of other individuals within a population. Each population must also connect to the ranges of other populations to ensure that inbreeding does not occur. In at least one population of lions in the Santa Ana River watershed, this is a real concern.

The Santa Ana Mountains lion population has been restricted or nearly cut off from other populations. A recent effort preserved the corridor that allows mountain lions to move between the Chino Hills and Santa Ana Mountains via Coal Canyon. Additional corridors must be protected and restored to allow lions to move south and east from the Santa Ana Mountains into the Palomar and Laguna ranges.

Efforts also must be maintained to protect lions from hunting, as these animals play an important role in controlling deer and rabbit populations. Recent attempts to open a lion season have failed but will not go away.

Exploring the native plant garden behind the Lytle Creek Ranger Station

away slowly, and let it pass. Snakes only bite when scared or threatened.

## Southern Oak Woodland

The southern oak woodland community dominates canyons and small valleys in the chaparral regions from just above sea level to 5000 feet elevation. The live oaks (coast, interior, and canyon) are the dominant tree species found here. Native grasses, ferns, and broadleaf evergreens such as toyon, lemonade berry, or holly-leaf cherry, often make up the understory of these woodlands, however, due to livestock grazing, invasive introduced annual grasses have replaced the native species in many places. At the bottom of canyons, the oaks are often joined by California sycamore and white alder as they transition into riparian woodland.

Many bird species can be found here, including red-shouldered and cooper's hawks. Oak titmice are common here, as are yellow-rumped warblers. Bobcats frequent this community, feeding on ground squirrels and rodents.

## Riparian Woodland

Immediately alongside the river and its tributary streams, we find riparian woodland. This important community can be found from sea level to above 10,000 feet and is composed of willows, cottonwoods, alders, sycamores, ashes, mulefat, and other trees and shrubs. Although this community is often found lining the river, it will grow wherever there is available water and it can form large, wooded areas, as it has behind Prado Dam in Corona, where it covers thousands of acres.

Because of the occurrence of water and the broad elevation range of this community, most of the wildlife species found in other communities also can be found here. In fact, at some point, nearly every animal visits the riparian zone. With patience, one is likely to see a variety of wildlife when visiting the riparian zone, from mountain lions and deer to rattlesnakes and rabbits.

**A black Phoebe rests at the Anaheim Wetlands.**

## Santa Ana Sucker

**STATUS:** Federally threatened

**DESCRIPTION:** This small fish (*Catostomus santaanea*) is less than 6 inches long and is usually brown on the back and silvery gray beneath. Irregular dark blotches also mark the back. The fish feeds on algae, detritus, and small insects collected from the cobbles along river and stream bottoms.

**LIFE CYCLE:** Santa Ana suckers begin to reproduce after they are a year old, though they do not often live to be older than 3. Spawning occurs from early April through July but peaks in May and June.

**HABITAT:** The Santa Ana sucker lives in Southern California streams and rivers with clean, clear, and cool water, though it also can survive seasonal turbidity. The streams cannot exceed 7 meters wide and 1 meter deep. These streams also must have small- and medium-cobble bottoms for the fish to feed off of.

**CONSERVATION:** Once considered common throughout its range, the Santa Ana sucker has undergone significant declines since at least the 1970s. Pollution due to urbanization and mining, water diversions and groundwater pumping, and introduced predators have all impacted the Santa Ana sucker. In addition, cattle and other livestock may have contributed to the decline through increased nitrification of stream flows.

The Santa Ana sucker has been considered in the Western Riverside Multi-Species Habitat Conservation Plan as well as other conservation agreements, however, a recent decision by the US Fish and Wildlife Service excludes all of the Santa Ana River populations from the critical habitat designated in the sucker's recovery plan.

---

Although the riparian community once was very common, today it has been reduced to a tiny fraction of its historic size. Agriculture, residential development, flood control, and water reclamation all have contributed to the reduction in riparian habitat. As a result, many rare, threatened, and endangered species are found in this community. Among these species are the least bells vireo, southwest willow flycatcher, and yellow warblers. Several fish species that once were common here now are endangered, including the arroyo chub, Santa Ana sucker, and three-spine stickleback.

# Coastal Sage Scrub

Coastal sage scrub once dominated much of the watershed's lower elevation, from sea level to 2500 feet. Due to intense development on the coastal plain and foothill areas, this community has been limited to a few protected areas and the upper foothills. This community is named for the dominant species of this community, coastal sagebrush (also commonly called California sagebrush), which is not a true sage; rather, it is a member of the sunflower family, similar to the one found throughout the Great Basin region. Cactus species, common buckwheat, many true sages, and California sunflower are other common members of this diverse community.

Alluvial sage scrub, a rare variation of coastal sage scrub, is found at the base of the San Bernardino Mountains. This community is subjected

## Santa Ana River Woolly Star

**STATUS:** Federally endangered

**DESCRIPTION:** Considered one of the most endangered plants in California, the Santa Ana River woolly star (*Eriastrum densifolium sanctorum*) is a perennial member of the phlox family and can grow to 3 feet high. The foliage of the plant is a distinguished gray-green. Its flowers are bright blue, tubular, and found in flower heads with as many as 20 flowers each.

**LIFE CYCLE:** The Santa Ana River woolly star is a perennial shrub that blooms from late May to early August.

**HABITAT:** Found on the sandy floodplain of the Santa Ana River in a vegetation community known as riversidian alluvial sage scrub, the species is restricted to an area between Seven Oaks Dam and Santa Ana River Regional Park in San Bernardino and Riverside counties.

**CONSERVATION:** The Santa Ana River woolly star is threatened by habitat conversion and altered flood regime. Perhaps the greatest threat to this species is the relatively new Seven Oaks Dam. The woolly star requires replenished sand deposits that likely will be restricted by the flood-control facility. The species is included in the Western Riverside Multi-Species Habitat Conservation Plan and other set aside areas, including the Santa Ana River Wash. Control of giant cane (*Arundo donax*) will improve the survivability of this spectacular wildflower.

to periodic flooding and is comprised mostly of evergreen species including yuccas. At first glance, this community appears more desert-like than coastal; however, it actually shares more characteristics with its coastal cousins than with its desert relatives.

California gnatcatchers, cactus wrens, and several reptiles are rare members of the animal kingdom that inhabit this community. This community is also the focus of the numerous multi-species habitat plans that have been developed to circumvent the strict guidelines of the Endangered Species Act.

## Marshland (Freshwater, Brackish, Saltwater)

Historically, much of the Santa Ana River watershed, especially the coastal plain, was marshland. As runoff from heavy rains increased flows in the river and its tributaries, water would escape historic channels flooding low-lying areas. Sometimes these areas would remain saturated for years, forming huge freshwater marshes. It is estimated that as many as 40,000 acres of the coastal plain were marsh at times.

Marsh vegetation consists primarily of cattails, bulrush, and various sedges. These dense, wet areas became important for wildlife, sheltering and feeding thousands of ducks, geese, and other waterfowl.

The Santa Ana River separated two large mash complexes in Orange County's history. To the east and south of the river was La Cienaga de las Ranas or Lake of the Frogs. To the west and north of the river was Gospel Swamp, named for the large, revival-style church gatherings that would occur there in the late 1800s and early 1900s. During years with heavy precipitation, these two wetlands covered more than 25,000 acres each. Today, only tiny pieces of these huge marshes remain.

The largest wetland area in the watershed today is in the Prado Basin, a 10,000-acre complex of mixed wetland types. The basin is mostly riparian forest, however, the Orange County Water District has, in the last decade, created hundreds of acres of treatment wetlands that improve water quality while also providing some habitat value. In addition, a great deal of mulefat scrub has been established to increase the habitat in the Prado Basin.

The marshes along the river closer to the ocean begin to mix with saltwater, and this habitat is referred to as brackish marsh. Brackish marshes also form where large amounts of minerals are deposited into the wetland by runoff. Salt grass is common in brackish marshes. Many species of waterfowl can be found in this community, including cinnamon teals, wood ducks, and buffle heads.

At some point, as freshwater mixes with ocean water, saltwater dominates the system and it becomes a saltwater marsh. Historically, the Santa Ana River emptied into two different saltwater marshes—Newport Bay and Bolsa Chica—however, these two complexes likely connected to one another at some point in history. There is evidence that the entire coastline between the two estuary complexes once was marshland, although most of it has been filled to support residential and commercial development.

Eel grass and cord grass are the most common plants in this habitat. Eel grass, an aquatic plant, can grow in 20 feet of water. Cord grass is the most common plant in saltwater marsh habitat and grows where only its roots are submerged for extended periods. This species is very important to the system because it breaks down and become detritus, which is fed on by many species of invertebrates that in turn feed birds, fish, and other wildlife.

Due to intensive development along the Southern California coast, many saltwater marshes have been filled or reduced, and this community now has numerous endangered species. Among them is the light-footed clapper rail, a narrow bird that evolved to maneuver through the sensitive marsh plants without disturbing them while feeding in the mud.

**Looking north from the Santa Ana River at the Talbert Marsh**

## Coastal Dune

The coastal dune or coastal strand is an area not inundated by surf or tidal submergence, where the constant onshore wind stacks up sand-forming mounds or "dunes." Common plants in this community include beach sagewort, sand verbena, beach primrose, beach morning glory, beach ragweed, and dune buckwheat.

The buckwheats are important in this area because they are the preferred nectar of several butterflies known as the blues, including the endangered Palos Verdes blue butterfly. The California least tern, an endangered bird, nests on small islands in marshes and estuaries often associated with coastal dune habitat.

Because of its size, geographic location, and elevation differences, the Santa Ana River watershed provides an excellent opportunity to observe, study, and experience the natural history of Southern California first hand. For those interested in learning more about the plants, animals, and geology of the Santa Ana River watershed, there are many excellent references and field guides available. I recommend Allan A. Schoenherr's *A Natural History of California* to get the interested reader going. In addition, many of the parks, reserves, and recreational facilities located along the river (and described in the following section of this book) provide formal and informal educational programs for little or no fee.

# CULTURAL HISTORY OF THE SANTA ANA RIVER

Throughout history, the Santa Ana River has sustained numerous cultures and communities, from the primitive hunter-gatherers to the most industrial and mechanical societies of the 21st century. This chapter is an introduction to these and every group in between that has cast its line into the river or sunk its roots into the soil of the watershed.

## Before European Contact

The earliest human evidence in the region dates back at least 12,000 years and is believed to be from nomadic people moving through the area hunting large prehistoric mammals such as camels, bison, and horses. Some experts believe these people were so efficient at killing their prey that they drove the large animals and eventually themselves into extinction. Changes in the region's climate, as temperatures grew hotter and the large inland lakes dried up, likely contributed significantly to the demise of the animals. By 6000 BC, the native people of Southern California had begun to settle in the area and diversified their lifestyle.

Over the next 3000 years, the people of the watershed became experts at fishing, fashioning fish hooks out of abalone shells and making line from yucca and cattail. Along the coast, line was twisted from seal sinew. They also speared fish in shallow pools using long poles with sharpened ends or stone points attached to them.

The first people to settle in the Santa Ana River watershed gathered seeds, berries, and fruit and developed stone tools for processing these

## Historically Important Events Along the Santa Ana River

**1542:** Juan Rodriguez Cabrillo sails past the mouth of the Santa Ana River prior to setting anchor off the Channel Island coast and becoming the first European to make contact with local Native Americans.

**1769:** Juan Gaspar de Portola becomes the first European to visit the Santa Ana River watershed when his party camped along Santiago Creek.

**1810:** A flood along the Santa Ana River is recorded for the first time.

**1825:** A major flood event forms the Balboa Peninsula as sediment is washed out of the mountains by the Santa Ana River.

**1903:** James Talbert forms the Newport Protection District, and the lower Santa Ana River is confined to a channel for the first time.

**1915:** Advocates first discuss the potential of the river to support a recreational trail corridor.

**1920:** The Santa Ana River is realigned to bypass Newport Bay when a new outlet is created at the boundary between Newport and Huntington beaches.

**1941:** Prado Dam is constructed.

**1999:** Seven Oaks Dam is constructed.

---

foods. The indigenous people of the Santa Ana River watershed collected as many as 200 species of plants for food, medicine and other uses.

Acorns were a staple source of nutrients and fiber. The natives would peel, grind, leach, and then dry the processed seeds of oaks. Once dried, they would use the material like flour or oatmeal. Blackberries, wild grapes, buckwheat, pine nuts, and elderberries were also commonly gathered and eaten raw, dried or roasted.

White sage, which they ground into a paste and used for medicine, was an important plant. The generic name of the sages is "salvia," which means "to heal." The plant was also bundled, dried, and burned like incense during ceremonies. This practice remains popular today with indigenous revivalists and New Age enthusiasts. White sage often can be found on the shelves of New Age bookstores.

The first people developed expertise in basketry, using deer grass, pine needles, and yucca fibers to weave beautiful, durable bowls, plates, and deep storage containers. Some baskets were woven tightly and coated with tar to hold water. The baskets of the first people in the watershed remain some of the finest in the world.

Ornamentation was important, and the people began to create figurines such as whales, dolphins, dogs, and birds. The small charms carved from steatite, a locally mined stone, have been found throughout the watershed, especially at archeological sites along the lower river and coast. Jewelry also was fashioned from shells and bones and regarded highly.

Another aspect of the natives' culture was ceremony, which was enhanced with songs and music. They carved instruments such as whistles and flutes from elderberry branches common in canyons and along the river and its tributaries. These people, like most of the native cultures of California, did not use drums in their songs or rituals. Instead, they kept the beat with clapper sticks and rattles.

This was a time of tribal development and territorial establishment. By 1500 AD, the native peoples of the Santa Ana River had settled into permanent villages or seasonal ones they would return to year after year. They developed complex religious practices and governmental organizations. They also had rituals to usher youth into adulthood or to scare evil spirits from the land. Their extensive mythology was passed down to new generations, and elaborate sand paintings were produced to praise their gods. They refined their art and ornamentation, including body adornment such as tattoos and piercing. Although both men and women were known to decorate themselves, women commonly tattooed their faces and upper bodies.

As many as 15,000 people representing four different tribal groups may have lived in the watershed at this time. All of the tribes spoke Uto-Aztecan or Shoshonean languages and are believed to have descended from people moving south along the Sierra Nevada Mountains, eventually populating regions as far south as Central America. These native groups are mostly recognized by their given names, not by what they call themselves, however, for purposes of recognition, this guide will refer to native groups by both names.

The Serranos, which meant "mountain people," called themselves the Yuharetum and settled in the San Bernardino Mountains and associated foothills up to around 7000 feet. The Luiseno, or Payomkowishum, were named after the Mission San Luis Rey, which they were forced to relocate to. They originally claimed the valleys between the east slope of the Santa Ana Mountains and the west slope of the San Jacintos. The Cahuilla (Kawia or Kaweah) made homes on the desert bajadas and passes to the southeast of the Yuharetum/Serranos and north of the Payomkowishum/Luiseno. The Los Angeles Basin, including most of what is now Orange County, was the territory of the Gabrielinos, people who were relocated to the Mission San Gabriel; they called themselves the Tongva.

The people of the watershed coexisted peacefully and shared many similarities not limited to their languages. Diets were similar for all of the tribes in the region, as is evident by the many bedrock mortars or grinding stones located throughout the Santa Ana River watershed. Diets differed most between coastal and desert groups. They shared similar stories of creation and all studied the sky in day and night. In fact, all the groups believed stars were connected to the "upper world" and feared falling stars, believing that each carried evil spirits to the earth.

A trading network developed that connected people all over Southern California. The coastal groups brought fish and shells to the east and acquired obsidian and pelts that were less available in the lower watershed. The groups would participate in each others ceremonies and feast together. There were even intertribal marriages.

## Spanish/Mexican Era

The lives of native people in the region changed drastically in 1769 when Juan Gaspar de Portola, a Spanish conquistador, and his party of soldiers and priests entered the lower watershed. The party camped on the banks of Santiago Creek and the Santa Ana River in what is now Orange County, claiming the area for the king of Spain.

They were not the first Europeans to see the watershed. Juan Rodriguez Cabrillo sailed past the mouth of the river in 1542. He landed on the Channel Islands off the coast of modern Ventura, but he never made for the mainland. Portola was, however, the first European to physically enter the Santa Ana River watershed. His party camped at the foot of the Santa Ana Mountains on Saint Anne's Day, and the party named the area the "Valley of Saint Anne."

The river was first named El Rio del Dulcissimo de Jesus de los Temblores, or the "River of the Sweetest Name of Jesus of Earthquakes," because there was a significant trembler the afternoon they camped there. The padres described it as a "great disruption" in which "everything shook" and the animals "cried." They even described the Santa

Ana River as changing course and flowing upstream for a few minutes before returning to its original path.

The expedition's soldiers felt the river's name was too cumbersome and opted instead for the title Rio de Santa Ana, believing that it flowed from the mountains they already had named for Saint Anne. The name for the river stuck, and the naming of the city and the hot, dry winds that follow the river's path came later and remain today.

With Portola were Franciscan missionaries. Father Junipero Serra was assigned to the expedition to establish missions, to help claim the territory for Spain, and to Christianize the "Indians." Serra started nine missions in California, including San Diego in 1769, San Gabriel in 1771, and San Juan Capistrano in 1776.

The Mission San Luis Rey was not established until 1798, but individuals that later would be grouped with the Luiseno were the first people in the Santa Ana watershed encountered by Portola and Serra. The Gabrielino and later the Serrano would follow. The Cahuilla did not encounter Europeans until 1774, when the Anza Expedition passed through the watershed on its way to Mission San Gabriel. The Anza Expedition was the first party to come to California and the Santa Ana River watershed on an overland route. Following the small 1774 Anza Expedition came a larger colonizing one in 1775–1776.

**De Anza Crossing marker at Martha McLean-Anza Narrows Regional Park**

With the establishment of the missions, life changed forever for the native people of the Santa Ana River. The people were forced to leave their villages and move to the missions, where there were required to do hard labor and disease overtook many. They were introduced to agriculture, adobe construction, and European clothing. Of course, the biggest change was worshiping the Catholic god and saints, and giving up a faith in Chinigchinich and other gods. They were forbidden from practicing their traditional religious ceremonies and from speaking their own languages, and they were limited in their freedom to gather seeds, nuts, and berries in a traditional manner. By the end of the mission period, most local tribes had all but lost their traditional lifestyles and historic knowledge of the watershed.

The Kawia/Cahuilla were a notable exception to this, as they were not forcibly relocated to the missions. The Spanish believed the deserts were to be avoided, and thus so were the people who lived there. The Kawia/Cahuilla had little contact with Europeans other than the passing of small groups until the 1840–50s.

The Spanish dominated the Santa Ana River watershed for more than the next 50 years, until 1833. Although there were no missions in the Santa Ana River watershed, both the San Gabriel and San Juan Capistrano missions had great influence over the lands there. An *asistencia* was established at modern-day San Bernardino to assist the San Gabriel Mission with its ranching and religious operations. Another mission outpost, established in what is today Costa Mesa, served the Mission San Juan Capistrano. However, control of the region by Spain and the Church was soon to end.

By 1834, Governor Jose Figueroa issued regulations for the emancipation of all mission Indians and the separation of land from the missions. The proclamation required that half the mission lands be given to the indigenous people. Few ever received title to any land, however, and most who did were tricked out of their holdings. Others who managed to hang onto their land tried to grow crops, but these efforts were mostly short-lived. The majority of the mission lands ended up going to those already holding large grants or ranchos in the region. Most of the mission Indians went to work on the ranchos or moved to the growing cities of the area.

Don Juan Pablo Grijalva, who came to the watershed with the first Anza Expedition, was the first person to stake a private claim in the watershed. In 1801, he petitioned the king of Spain for approximately 62,500 acres of land along the eastern shore of the Santa Ana River. The land became known as Rancho Santiago de Santa Ana and was the only

Spanish rancho in the watershed. The other ranchos in Alta California were deeded during Mexican rule. Grijalva died in 1806, leaving the rancho to his wife, Maria Dolores Valencia, and grandsons, Antonio Yorba and Juan Peralta.

The Yorba and Peralta names have been applied to many places in the watershed, including the Peralta Hills and city of Yorba Linda. The rancho would include the first adobe building outside the missions. At one time, there may have been as many as 30 adobe structures on the Rancho Santiago de Santa Ana.

Several towns were established within the ranchos, and Rancho Santiago de Santa Ana was no exception. The "Santa Ana Arriba," or Upper Santa Ana town site is located just north of the Peralta Hills and is home to the Peralta Adobe. Downstream of the hills is "Santa Ana Vieja," or Old Santa Ana. This was the main town of the Rancho Santiago de Santa Ana. A historical marker (#204) designates the site at Lincoln and Orange-Olive roads in the city of Orange. The site of the Yorba Hacienda overlooked the location of the town, which once included stores, banks, and even an elected mayor. "Santa Ana Abajo," or Lower Santa Ana, an extension of Santa Ana Vieja, was located downstream, near where Chapman Ave. now crosses the river. This was the historic crossing of El Camino Real and remains a major crossing of the river today.

Many ranchos were granted during the Mexican period and stretched from the foot of the San Bernardino Mountains to the coast. Following separation of land from the missions in 1833, most land on the banks of the Santa Ana was added to existing rancho grants. Included among these were Rancho San Bernardino, Rancho Las Bolsas, San Juan Cajon de Santa Ana, Santa Ana del Chino, Canon de Santa Ana, La Sierra de Yorba, El Rincon, La Sierra Sepulveda, and Jurupa.

Life on the ranchos was full and exciting. Most raised cattle and horses and grew a few crops. The Californios, as the rancho families became known, were a proud bunch. The men heading up the ranchos had military backgrounds, and many had come with the first European expeditions into the region. They raised large families and stayed in close contact with one another.

On the bluffs above the river's mouth was an outpost that served the Mission San Juan Capistrano prior to 1833. This small adobe was constructed between 1817 and 1823 to house soldiers and ranch hands who watched over the mission's cattle and a Tongva/Gabrielino village just below. The view from this estancia was impressive, overlooking miles of coastline and much of the gently rolling grasslands that make up what are now Costa Mesa, Santa Ana, and Huntington Beach.

In 1827, the padres at Mission San Juan Capistrano considered relocating the entire mission to the estancia site because water was more abundant and the grazing lands were richer. The move never happened, but the estancia continued to grow in size and importance.

When the mission era ended, the estancia became property of Don Jose Diego Sepulveda. At one time, Sepulveda owned more than 100,000 acres, including the Rancho San Joaquin. He became quite rich raising cattle and racing horses, however, he spent as quickly as he collected. Eventually, he lost all but the El Refugio, a 1000-acre horse ranch carved from the center of the original Rancho Santiago de Santa Ana.

El Refugio is believed to have been somewhere below the confluence of Santiago Creek and the Santa Ana River in modern-day Santa Ana. Known for its extravagance, El Refugio was the site of many fiestas, rodeos, and bull vs. bear fights. The main building is thought to have been the grandest of all adobes built in the watershed.

Although the Californios rose to wealth and power during Spanish rule, by 1822, Mexico had taken control of Alta California. The Mexican government, controlled by the country's elite, showed little interest in Alta California. It was too far away, and they had plenty of problems close to home. This bothered the rancheros, but ultimately benefited

**Relaxing in the shade of the Diego Sepulveda Adobe**

them, as they were not impacted by the violence occurring in Mexico proper. Life continued along the Santa Ana River as it had for the past 25 years.

Visitors from the east passed through the area, most in search of furs, but others with an eye on territory. Jedediah Smith explored the watershed in 1826, crossing the San Bernardino and Santa Ana mountains before spending some time as a "prisoner" at the San Gabriel Mission. Kit Carson entered the San Bernardinos in 1830 but did not stay long. It was, of course, the presence of John C. Fremont that made the Mexicans most nervous, and rightly so. He was in the watershed seeking territory for the US.

After the Bear Flag Revolt in 1846, and the Mexican American War, which lasted through 1848, the area was stripped from Mexico and became a free republic, then a US state in 1850. One story puts the Santa Ana River at the heart of the battle for California.

Following the raising of the bear flag in Sonoma, which gave the Bear Flag Revolt its name, the Bear Flaggers rode for Los Angeles, where small skirmishes between Mexico and the California Republicans continued. Here, a small band of American rebels was out-gunned by Mexican loyalists; however, due to the heavy flows in the Santa Ana River at that time, larger reinforcements could not cross at Chino to continue pushing the rebels back north. This allowed the Americans to regroup and maintain their command of the region. By 1848, Mexico had conceded Alta California.

Although many of the rancheros supported American rule, the presence of another distant government would not suit them. With the discovery of gold in Northern California, the lifestyle of the Californio was soon to end. Although separated from the Gold Rush of the Sierra Nevada foothills, new settlers began pouring into the watershed seeking their fortunes. At first, the demand for cattle was great and the ranchos prospered.

These new settlers, mostly Americans, started small farms, irrigating their crops with water from the Santa Ana River. New towns sprung up. Among these were San Bernardino, started by Mormons in 1851, and Anaheim in 1859.

In 1860, gold was discovered in the San Bernardino Mountains and thousands rushed to the high country. Within days of William Holcomb's find, claims were placed throughout the range. Although the strike was outside the Santa Ana River drainage, the watershed was to play an important role in the mining boom. New towns were built and lumber was needed. Large logging operations began and the slopes were clear-cut. Small railroad operations were constructed to haul the trees and lumber. Several mills were established to process the lumber.

As the populations grew, lumber was hauled down the mountains as well as to the mines in the high country. At one point, more people lived in the San Bernardino Mountains than in the rest of San Bernardino County combined. The town of Bellville in the Holcomb Valley was estimated to have had as many as 10,000 residents at its peak. It almost became the county seat of San Bernardino, losing to the Mormon city of San Bernardino by only two votes.

Placer mining occurred in the 1860s in Lytle Creek, but neither the Holcomb Valley nor Lytle Creek gold fields ever produced much profitable gold. Many geologists and mine enthusiasts believe the main gold vein has yet to be uncovered, and much wealth remains buried deep in the San Bernardino Mountains. Some small mines still operate today.

In 1862, the Santa Ana River flooded. Due in part to the intensive logging that was occurring upstream, huge debris flows came down the river, temporarily destroying much of the lower grazing land and washing away some of the small towns and settlements that had grown from within the ranchos.

Perhaps the most notable of these lost towns were La Placita and Agua Mansa, both established by 1842. These small towns were settled by Mexicans on opposite sides of the river between the modern cities of Colton and Riverside. The settlements were within the Jurupa Rancho owned by Juan Bandini, who welcomed them with the condition they watched over his herds and protect them from banditos and rogue Indian bands. Both towns were well-managed and respected for their order and visual quality. Each was built in the river bottom, which in this area was quite wide and distant from the active channel.

The flood of 1862 is estimated to be the greatest flow known to have come down the river, topping more than 300,000 cubic feet per second. When it reached the towns, it completely engulfed them, killing more than 40 people. Today, only the Agua Mansa graveyard remains to remind people of the dangers of living in the floodplain.

Following the flood was the drought of 1863–1864. Some estimates claim that as many as 65,000 head of cattle and 35,000 horses died due to a lack of forage. This was enough to force many of the ranchos to dissolve or significantly reduce their holdings. Large-scale cattle grazing was abandoned in the region as an economic enterprise. Only small herds remained, and these were pushed into the mountains and foothills. Row crops and other plant-based agriculture replaced the ranching enterprises. Grapes, corn, beans, and melons were among these early crops.

In 1869, the California Silk Center Association was formed following the purchase of approximately 10,000 acres from the Jurupa and Rubidoux ranchos for producing silk. Mulberry trees were planted and silk worms were imported. But in 1870, Luis Prevost, president of the company and the only one with knowledge of the silk industry, died. The company ceased its silk production and focused its attention on grapes and eventually citrus. Numerous mulberry trees still grow in the area as a reminder of the short-lived Silk Center. Eventually, the land of the Silk Center became the city of Riverside.

In 1865, President Abraham Lincoln, through executive order, gave the missions at San Juan and San Gabriel back to the Catholic Church. The locations that once ruled Southern California never regained the vast land holdings they had managed, but the Church remained an important part life in early California.

By 1868, the Rancho Santiago de Santa Ana was partitioned, with pieces going to more than 100 heirs and a host of creditors. Many of the other ranchos already had dissolved or soon would. It was difficult for many of the rancho families to confirm their grants with the US government, and even when they could, the process often lasted more than a decade and became very expensive.

## Agricultural Era

The modern city of Santa Ana was founded in 1869 on what was the Rancho Santiago de Santa Ana. The town's location was just 10 miles south of Old Santa Ana (Santa Ana Viejo), which once existed along the banks of the river in the rancho. Twenty years later, the city was chosen as the seat of Orange County when it seceded from Los Angeles County in 1889. By that time, the Santa Fe Railroad had already reached Orange County and was hauling supplies in and crops out every week.

Coal and silver had been discovered in the Santa Ana Mountains a year earlier, and thousands were again trying their hands at the dream of quick riches from hard rock. The boomtowns of Carbondale and Silverado were established, complete with saloons, a jail, and several hotels.

However, not all was good in the watershed. The city of Riverside was established in 1870 on the former site of the Silk Center, which had fallen into failing financial conditions. The grape blight had struck and the wine and raisin industries were failing in the region. The Anaheim

Colony was particularly hard hit; thousands of acres of vineyards were devastated, and many farmers lost everything they had.

Another fruit, however, would save the day for the farmers of the Santa Ana River watershed. In 1873, two navel orange trees were shipped to the farm of Eliza Tibbets in Riverside by the US Agriculture Department. The trees thrived in the rich alluvial soil and warm sunshine of the area, and soon there were thousands of orange, lemon, and grapefruit trees throughout the watershed. Citrus remained the king of Southern California agriculture for the next 75 years until it began to be replaced by housing.

The citrus industry was so big in the lower watershed that the founding fathers of Orange County chose the prolific fruit to represent the county by name. It's estimated that by 1900, more than 150,000 navel and Valencia orange trees were growing in Orange County. However, other crops also were grown on the loams of the Santa Ana River floodplain in the lower watershed, including walnuts, avocados, sugar beets, strawberries, lima beans, and melons.

## Modern Era

In the first decade of the 1900s, human influences began to impact the river in ways they never had before. Water was being diverted to fields for agriculture and hundreds of wells were drilled to provide domestic water for the growing communities of the region. Dozens of water districts were founded to manage the acquisition and distribution of Santa Ana River water. Dams were built to generate electricity and to store water. The era of engineering had begun.

In 1938, the Santa Ana River again broke free of its levees and flooded thousands of acres. The communities below Santa Ana Canyon suffered the greatest damage. It is estimated that nearly 100,000 cubic feet per second of water roared down the upper river and through Santa Ana Canyon, opening up and washing over the cities of Anaheim, Santa Ana, Garden Grove, and Huntington Beach. The flood was responsible for the deaths of 58 people and more than $12 million in damage. In the middle of the night on March 3, a wall of water 6 to 8 feet high washed through and out of the canyon, crushing everything in its path. Much of the damage and loss of life occurred in the Mexican immigrant communities of Atwood and La Jolla, where dozens of homes were destroyed and nearly 40 people were killed.

The 1938 flood ushered in the first major modern engineering project on the Santa Ana River, the Prado Dam. The project actually was

The second Bear Valley Dam at the west end of Big Bear Lake

conceived decades prior and was approved in 1936, two years before the flood. In order to build the dam, much of the land behind it had to be purchased, and this was no small task. An entire town and numerous farms rested in the inundation zone.

By 1938, most of the village of Prado already was abandoned; its residents knew for years that the water was coming. However, a few shop owners and dairy operations remained to the very end. Established a century earlier as Rincon, the town changed its name in 1890 to appease the Santa Fe Railroad, which would not stop there because the company already had a stop named Rincon somewhere else. The town opted to call itself Prado after one of the early pioneers in the area; however, many of the town's residents referred to the village as Rincon well into the 1900s.

The village of Rincon, meaning corner or angle, sat where the Chino Hills and Santa Ana Mountains meet and the river takes a turn and angles toward the ocean. The settlement saw two spikes in population growth. The first occurred around 1885, when the town was marketed heavily as an agricultural paradise. The population went up again around 1905, as the railroad presence increased. By 1925, the cities of Corona and Riverside had overtaken the little village as a center of commerce and only a few potters and dairies remained in Prado. More than 200 historic and prehistoric sites lay buried beneath the waters of Prado Basin today.

The human population of the Santa Ana River watershed continued to grow during the first half of the 20th century. A post-World War II building boom began the conversion of large agricultural operations to housing and commercial development projects. Subdivisions replaced orange groves, and irrigation ditches dried up. Now the Santa Ana River, especially below Prado Dam, was viewed primarily as a conveyor of floodwaters.

Prado Dam helped ease concerns over the Santa Ana River's potential to flood more than 110,000 acres of Orange County and cause an estimated $15 billion in damage. US Army Corps of Engineers estimate that as many as 3000 deaths could be caused if the Santa Ana River were to break free of its levees and channel. Over the three decades following completion of Prado Dam, the river has only threatened to flood, but the earthen plug at the foot of Santa Ana Canyon held tight.

Then, in 1969, the Santa Ana River watershed again roared to life. This time, much of the damage was on tributaries such as San Timoteo and Santiago creeks. The reminder was clear—the Santa Ana River is a powerful force and has the potential to do great damage. Along lower Santiago Creek, the Marines helicoptered in old cars to help stabilize the banks, and hundreds of volunteers filled and placed sand bags. This was not enough to solve the problem, however, as homes just above the creek's confluence with the Santa Ana River lost patios, swimming pools, and garages to the rising swell of floodwaters.

In the 1960s, the US Army Corps of Engineers were declaring the Santa Ana River to be the greatest flood threat west of the Mississippi River. With this declaration, county flood-control agencies, state resource officers, and Congress finally saw a way to "remove" the threat, and the Santa Ana River Mainstem Project was born. The project, which aims to protect the residential and commercial property of the middle and lower watershed, is a huge undertaking of engineering tasks. In 1998, the Seven Oaks Dam was constructed at the foot of the San Bernardino Mountains. It is designed to hold back a 300-year rain event from washing over San Bernardino, Colton, and Riverside.

The only other dam on the river, Prado Dam, is getting a facelift and is being raised an additional 30 feet, with new gate structures and outlet works. Orange County Flood Control and the Army Corps of Engineers have designed the facilities to meet an estimated 190-year storm event. In addition, much of the river's levies have been reinforced with concrete and steel or riprap, and a new dike has been constructed to protect various structures, communities, and other features along the river.

In the time between 1969 and the initiation of the Mainstem Project in the 1990s, development continued. The three counties that comprise the watershed often topped the list of fastest-growing communities in the nation. Houses sprung up on hillsides where orange trees once grew, and, practically overnight, bean fields and vineyards were converted to concrete box buildings and industrial centers. Manufacturing facilities, factories, and retail centers were constructed on the banks of the river.

Unfortunately, the river was rarely embraced in this process. Mostly, buildings and walls separated the river from the view of passers-by as well as those entering the buildings on her banks. By the dawn of the 21st century, the river was forgotten by all but a small group of visionaries who could see, buried beneath concrete and confined between levee walls, the potential of this river to again be the center of life in the region. Thus, the Santa Ana River renaissance was born, as various government agencies began working with the Wildlands Conservancy to reconnect people to the river.

# GETTING TO, IN, AND ON THE RIVER

*left:* **At play on the river near Hidden Valley Wildlife Area in Riverside**

# RIVER REACHES

In this book, the Santa Ana River is divided into six sections:

The first section, the **San Bernardino Mountains Reach**, begins at the highest point of the river in the San Gorgonio Wilderness and Big Bear Valley and continues to the river's abrupt halt at the Seven Oaks Dam. Here, the river is bordered by alders and willows and has the feel of a clean and pristine mountain stream. The river itself is fast, cold, and crisp.

As the river escapes the confines of Seven Oaks Dam, it enters the **Santa Ana River Wash and Upper Inland Empire Reach**. Here, the river enters a broad, open, and flat bed of boulders and smaller cobbles. The alders of the high country give way to juniper, yucca, sage, and an occasional willow or mulefat shrub.

As the river crosses under Hwy. 60, it enters the **Santa Ana River Regional Park and Lower Inland Empire Reach**, one of the largest and most diverse reaches of the river. This area shares some characteristics with the reach above it, however, it is home to a more mature willow woodland and its water supply is of greater volume due to the addition of runoff from nearby treatment facilities and factories. This section has the feel of many rivers in the Southeast, as the broad, shallow, slow-moving river meanders toward the ocean. The name of this reach, which terminates at Prado Dam, is derived from the large areas managed by the Riverside County Regional Parks and Open-Space District; however, San Bernardino County Parks and the city of Riverside also manage property in this reach.

As the river tumbles free of Prado Dam, it enters the **Santa Ana Canyon Reach**, tucked between the Santa Ana Mountains and the Chino Hills. The river narrows here and becomes deeper. Lined by

*left:* **The Santa Ana River in the San Bernardino Mountains**

51

Reach I:   San Bernardino Mountains
Reach II:  Santa Ana River Wash and Upper Inland Empire
Reach III: Santa Ana River Regional Park and Lower Inland Empire:
           Highway 60 to Prado Dam
Reach IV:  Santa Ana Canyon
Reach V:   Orange County Coastal Plain
Reach VI:  Orange Coast and the River Mouth

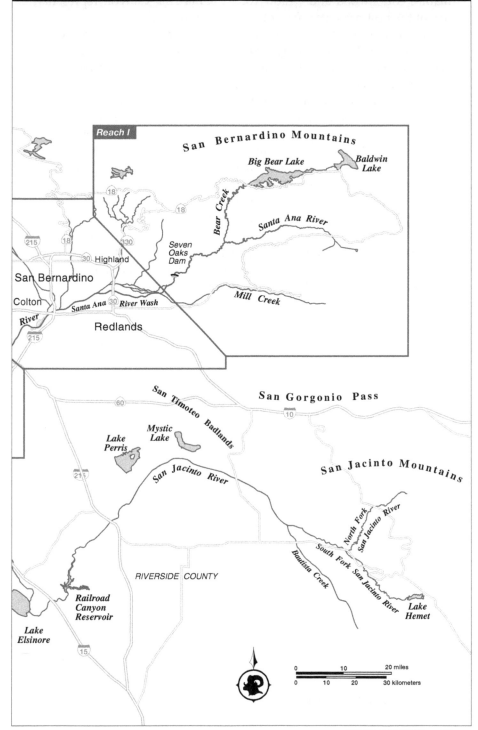

mature cottonwood and willow forest, Santa Ana Canyon represents one of the best presentations of the river environment.

At the mouth of Santa Ana Canyon, the river exits the fourth reach and enters the **Orange County Coastal Plain Reach**. Here, the river has been completely channeled, save for the numerous diversions to groundwater recharge settling ponds in its upper section. This is the most urban section of the Santa Ana River, but it is also my favorite. This is where most people who visit the river live and make contact with it. Some estimates place 10,000 "users" on this reach on any given weekend day. There are many small parks and open space areas along this reach, and it is also home to the most complete section of bike trail on the river, stretching from Santa Ana Canyon to the ocean.

The **Orange Coast and the River Mouth Reach** is the final reach and the only one that includes an ocean. Though the river remains channeled at this location, it appears more open and natural as it mixes with the ocean and empties into the blue Pacific. In addition to the parks that line the river here, the historic outlets and marshes of the river are also described, even though they are today, miles from the river.

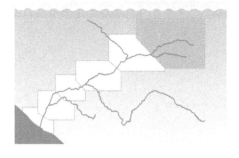

# SAN BERNARDINO MOUNTAINS

"Old Grayback" is what, for the last century, locals have called 11,502-foot San Gorgonio Mountain. It is also where the Santa Ana River begins. As snow melts from the highest peak in Southern California, some of the water trickles to the north, forming the main and South Fork of the Santa Ana River. This often icy stretch of the river is understandably the most pristine. Wild, fast-moving, narrow, and covered by a dense woodland canopy, the river here is rich in wildlife, including rainbow trout, mule deer, black bear, bobcat, and many species of birds.

Tall, straight, white alders stand along the banks of the river, interrupted only by the occasional small willow or black cottonwood. Pines, including Jeffrey and ponderosa, mix with oaks and incense-cedars to form the forest that surrounds the river and covers the north-facing slopes of its upper canyon.

Farther north, in the Big Bear Valley, Bear Creek forms an unofficial "north fork" of the Santa Ana. Falling rapidly from the Bear Valley Dam and Big Bear Lake, Bear Creek is a rugged and wild stream, though it is obviously influenced by water releases from the Bear Valley Dam. From the dam, Bear Creek cascades rapidly, carving a forested canyon to its confluence with the Santa Ana River a few miles above the Seven Oaks Dam.

The San Gorgonio section of the river's headwaters forms a wilderness playground, rich with trails, camps, and scenic beauty. The Bear Valley area is also home to outstanding natural scenery; however, it is more developed and is geared toward activities such as boating, skiing,

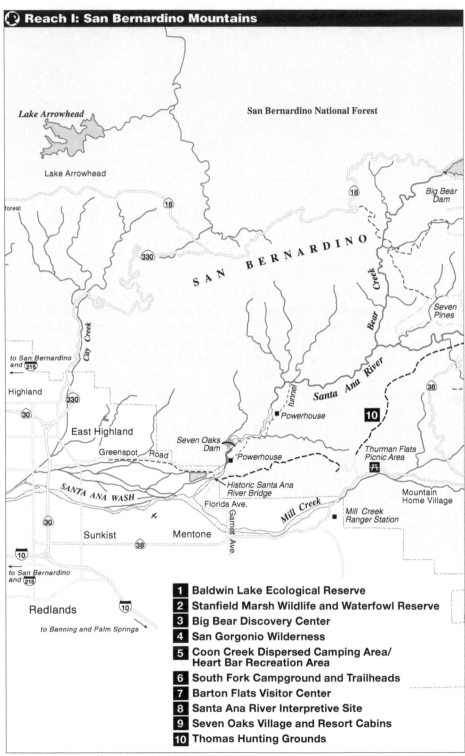

Lake Arrowhead

San Bernardino National Forest

Lake Arrowhead

forest

Big Bear Dam

San Bernardino National Forest

S A N  B E R N A R D I N O

City Creek

Bear Creek

Seven Pines

to San Bernardino and 215

Highland

East Highland

Greenspot Road

Santa Ana River

tunnel

Powerhouse

Seven Oaks Dam

Powerhouse

Thurman Flats Picnic Area

SANTA ANA WASH

Historic Santa Ana River Bridge

Florida Ave.

Mill Creek

Mountain Home Village

Mill Creek Ranger Station

Sunkist

Mentone

Garnet Ave.

to San Bernardino and 215

Redlands

to Banning and Palm Springs

**1** Baldwin Lake Ecological Reserve

**2** Stanfield Marsh Wildlife and Waterfowl Reserve

**3** Big Bear Discovery Center

**4** San Gorgonio Wilderness

**5** Coon Creek Dispersed Camping Area/ Heart Bar Recreation Area

**6** South Fork Campground and Trailheads

**7** Barton Flats Visitor Center

**8** Santa Ana River Interpretive Site

**9** Seven Oaks Village and Resort Cabins

**10** Thomas Hunting Grounds

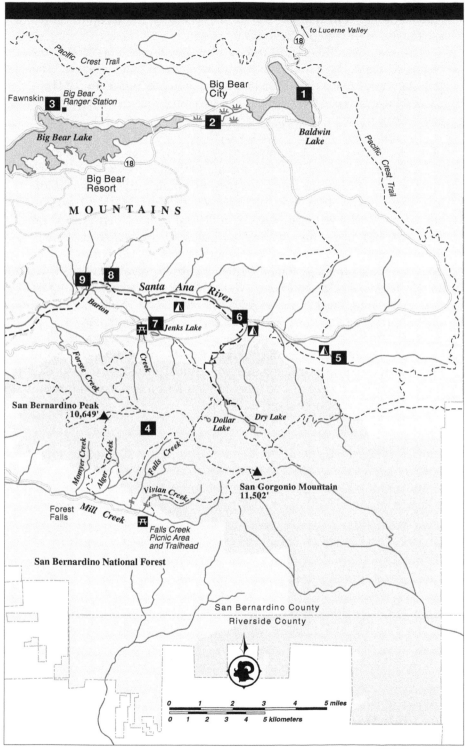

to Lucerne Valley

18

Pacific Crest Trail

Big Bear
City

**1**

Fawnskin
Big Bear
Ranger Station

**3**

**2**

Baldwin
Lake

Pacific Crest Trail

*Big Bear Lake*

18

Big Bear
Resort

**M O U N T A I N S**

**9**  **8**

*Santa  Ana  River*

Barton

**7**  *Jenks Lake*

**6**

Creek

**5**

Forsee Creek

San Bernardino Peak
10,649'

**4**

Monver Creek

Alger Creek

Falls Creek

Dollar
Lake

Dry Lake

Vivian Creek

San Gorgonio Mountain
11,502'

Forest
Falls

Mill  Creek

Falls Creek
Picnic Area
and Trailhead

**San Bernardino National Forest**

San Bernardino County
Riverside County

0    1    2    3    4    5 miles

0   1   2   3   4   5 kilometers

and shopping. Both areas are within the San Bernardino National Forest and are mostly on public lands.

The Santa Ana River Trail through the San Bernardino Mountains begins where the river does, on the north slope of Old Grayback. The trail stays close to the river from its starting point to its crossing of Hwy. 38. Just beyond the highway, the trail rises above the river and hugs the south slope of Santa Ana Canyon.

The trail doesn't make contact with the river again until it drops out of the San Bernardino Mountains. Instead, it stays high above the river in the shade of often thick conifer forests. Occasionally, the trail crosses open, meadow-like grasslands rich in native bunch grasses, microbiotic crusts, and wildflowers. Manzanitas, chinquapins, and willow shrubs grow where the soil and its moisture content permit. Several Forest Service roads cross the trail, and most lead to the river at some point, making loop trips of various lengths possible. The Forest Service does not allow camping along the river, except in private facilities such as Seven Oaks Lodge and Seven Oaks Mountain Cabins. The closest remote camping must be done north of Forest Road 1N04 or at any of several primitive "yellow post" sites described in this chapter.

Adventure Passes, part of a fee-based program to generate funding for all four Southern California national forests, are required for many of the locations described in this section. Annual passes sell for $30, day passes are $5, and they can be purchased at Forest Service visitor centers, sporting goods stores, and outfitters.

# Baldwin Lake Ecological Reserve

**HIGHLIGHTS:** Discover plants so small you need a magnifying glass to see what they are.

**ACCESS:** Baldwin Lake can be accessed at the intersection of Hwy. 18 and Holcomb Valley Road.

**SEASON & HOURS:** Open all year from sunrise to sunset but it may be snowed in or frozen in winter.

**FACILITIES:** Informational displays, trails, and a boat launch.

**CONTACT:** California Department of Fish and Game: 909-597-9823; www.dfg.ca.gov/er/region6/baldwin.

Baldwin Lake, the biggest natural lake in the San Bernardino Mountains, can be as large as several hundred acres, but it varies in size from

**Hiking the shore at Baldwin Lake**

*Photo by Bobby Palmer*

year to year due to the amount of snow melt the valley receives. Expanding and decreasing lake levels also change the amount of the reserve accessible to the public, making repeated visits to Baldwin Lake worthwhile. The Baldwin Lake Ecological Reserve protects approximately 60 acres.

The lake formed during the last ice age, when clay deposits developed under heavy peat and other debris in the valley. The clay soil of the lakebed has frozen and thawed thousands of times, and as it does, tiny quartz pebbles are forced up through the clay and deposited on the surface. Areas where this has occurred are known as "pebble plains" and are home to an amazing array of tiny endemic plants.

The rare plants found here are just some of the many exciting discoveries that await visitors to the Baldwin Lake Ecological Reserve. Spring through autumn are the best seasons to see waterfowl at Baldwin Lake, though it is possible to spot American coots in winter trying to walk on the frozen waters of the lake. In late autumn and winter, bald eagles congregate in the Big Bear Valley and sometimes hunt in and around Baldwin Lake. Small boats are allowed on the water and are the best ways to view the birds that congregate in the interior of the lake. Hunting is allowed by boat only, but check with the California Department of Fish and Game for seasons, limits, and permits.

Whenever you come to Baldwin Lake Ecological Reserve, the experience promises to be a memorable one, so be sure to pack a camera and binoculars and dress for a variety of weather conditions, as the high country of the Big Bear Valley can change quickly. Snow in September and 80°F days in February are not out of the question.

# Stanfield Marsh Wildlife and Waterfowl Reserve

**HIGHLIGHTS:** Watch bald eagles fish at the Stanfield Marsh.

**ACCESS:** The Stanfield Marsh is located at the corner of Stanfield Cutoff and Big Bear Blvd. in the town of Big Bear Lake.

**SEASON & HOURS:** Open all year from sunrise to sunset, but parking may be snowed in during winter.

**FACILITIES:** Restrooms, interpretive displays, and a boardwalk-style trail.

**CONTACT:** Big Bear Valley Municipal Water District: 909-866-5796; www.bbmwd.org.

Depending on precipitation, the Stanfield Marsh Wildlife and Waterfowl Reserve might be a dry lakebed or completely submerged and contiguous with Big Bear Lake. Mostly, it is somewhere in between and it is always spectacular.

**Looking northeast across Stanfield Marsh**

Surrounded by majestic mountain peaks and lined with willows, sedges, and other wetland species, the 145-acre reserve guarantees a glimpse of the wild side of the Big Bear Valley. The area is home to a tremendous diversity of plants and animals; in fact, there are more than 125 species of plants per acre here—a diversity that can only be equaled by traveling the coast of North America from Baja to Canada.

Originally set aside as a reserve in 1982 by the Big Bear Valley Municipal Water District, the site has been expanded and enhanced since the water district partnered with the Natural Heritage Foundation in 1992. A predator-free island protected by a moat was constructed in the middle of the reserve to provide safe nesting for the many birds that use the area, including mallards, grebes, teals, and white pelicans. Osprey and bald eagles are also frequent visitors.

All of this natural diversity and beauty can be seen from the raised boardwalk that runs along the southern edge of the reserve and also serves as a safe route for pedestrians traveling along Big Bear Blvd. An interpretive kiosk is located near the parking lot, and benches provide visitors with comfortable viewing of wild Big Bear Valley.

# Big Bear Discovery Center

**HIGHLIGHTS:** The center has a friendly staff with lots of information, and it's also great for people watching, as many tourists come through the center.

**ACCESS:** 42300 North Shore Drive (also called Hwy. 38), Fawnskin.

**SEASON & HOURS:** Summer: 8 AM to 6 PM; winter: 8:30 AM to 5 PM.

**FACILITIES:** Restrooms, interpretive displays, trails, and store.

**CONTACT:** Big Bear Discovery Center: 909-382-2790; www.bigbeardiscoverycenter.com.

The Big Bear Discovery Center, an interpretive and information center at the north edge of Big Bear Lake, is well-staffed with knowledgeable Forest Service personnel and volunteers who welcome the opportunity to share with you their extensive information on great local hikes, current flowers in bloom, or even where to get a decent meal in the valley. Various displays depict the natural and cultural history of the area, while more information can be obtained through the hundreds of informational and promotional pamphlets available at the center.

**The biggest bear in Big Bear Valley**

*Photo by Bobby Palmer*

In addition to the interpretive information, there is a gift shop and a bookstore that offers several hard-to-find field guides, as well as books on the area and a wide variety of souvenirs. Refreshments can be purchased in the store, and there is a comfortable patio overlooking the lake that provides shaded picnic tables with great views of the surrounding mountains and lake.

Many short hikes and interpretive trails start nearby, making the center's extensive parking lot a nice staging area for casual adventures into the forest or along the lake. The Woodland Nature Trail is a short interpretive trail that begins just off the center's parking lot and is fully accessible to strollers and wheelchairs. The facility's staff can also provide information on longer hikes around the forest.

## Big Bear Mountain Resort

Considered Southern California's most complete mountain resort, Big Bear Mountain (909-866-5766) is really two separate operations. Located above the south shore of the lake in the town of Big Bear Lake, Bear Mountain and Snow Summit are primarily winter operations.

Bear Mountain is a winter extreme park, with some of the region's most adventurous jumps, jibs, and terrain. It is also home to the area's only giant halfpipe and it has the region's highest lift-served slopes, at more than 8800 feet.

Snow Summit is as laid back as Bear Mountain is extreme. In fact, it's possible to explore a huge portion of the mountain without returning to the base. The resort offers runs for all levels of skiers and boarders.

Both resorts offer instruction, food, and other services. In the summer, visitors can use the lifts to access mountain biking and hiking trails on the resort.

# San Gorgonio Wilderness

**HIGHLIGHTS:** On a clear day, you can see from Mexico to the Sierra Nevada, and from the Mojave Desert to the Pacific Ocean from the peak of San Gorgonio Mountain.

**ACCESS:** The San Gorgonio Wilderness can be accessed from many locations, but to be close to the river, the best access points are off of Hwy. 38, approximately 20 miles north of Redlands.

**SEASON & HOURS:** The wilderness area can be explored any time. However, all overnight stays require a wilderness permit, and an Adventure Pass is required for most parking areas that access the wilderness. Both can be obtained at the Mill Creek Ranger Station (909-382-2882) or, in summer, at the Barton Flats Visitor Center (909-794-4861).

**FACILITIES:** Trails. Some parking areas and trailheads may also have restrooms and interpretive displays.

**CONTACT:** Mill Creek Ranger Station: 909-382-2882.

Visitors can access the 95,000-acre San Gorgonio Wilderness from many locations, but for the purpose of seeing the Santa Ana River and its headwaters, it's best to enter the wilderness from Hwy. 38, where you will find access to more than 100 miles of trails, as well as many trailheads, campgrounds, and parking areas.

**Entering San Gorgonio Wilderness off the South Fork Trail**

**San Gorgonio Mountain from Dry Lake**

One option for a hike is to take the South Fork Trail to Dry Lake, which is 16 miles round trip. The trailhead is located a few miles southwest of Hwy. 38 on Jenks Lake Road, a loop road that connects to Hwy. 38 east and west of the Barton Flats area. The South Fork Trailhead is located near the middle of Jenks Lake Road, and the trail begins just across the road from the parking area. Dry Lake is the beginning of the South Fork of the Santa Ana River. The glacially constructed lowland here is sometimes dry, hence its name, but usually it is drowned by a shallow pool that reflects the forest and high peaks surrounding it. Lodgepole Spring is also located here.

San Gorgonio Mountain, a.k.a "Old Grayback," is the highest mountain in Southern California, reaching an elevation of 11,502 feet, and you can hike to its summit from numerous trailheads, including the South Fork Trailhead described above. Eight other peaks in this wilderness top 10,000 feet, making it a peak bagger's playground. The San Gorgonio Wilderness Association even sponsors the "Nine Peaks Challenge." Those who climb all nine can purchase a patch and "join" the Nine Peaks Club. A map of these peaks is available at the Mill Creek Ranger Station (909-382-2882).

For those who aren't up for that challenge, there are plenty of opportunities for solitude and relaxation in the San Gorgonio Wilderness. Mountain meadows, lakes, and deep forests abound. The waters that feed the lakes here also provide for vast forests of ponderosa and Jeffrey pines, which cover the gentler slopes and valley floors. A few meadows dot the landscape within the wilderness and provide showy wildflower displays into late summer. Higher up, the San Gorgonio Wilderness supports lodgepole pine and ancient limber pine. Those seeking the high-country environment more often associated with the Sierra Nevada can find plenty of steep gray granite here.

# Coon Creek Dispersed Camping Area/ Heart Bar Recreation Area

**HIGHLIGHTS:** Enjoy the luxury of car camping close to the river's headwaters.

**ACCESS:** To get to Heart Bar campground from the Mill Creek Ranger Station, follow Hwy. 38 north for 24 miles to Forest Road 1N02 and look for the sign for the campground. Turn right. To get to Coon Creek, continue on Forest Road 1N02 for about 4 more miles past Heart Bar campground.

**SEASON & HOURS:** Open May 15 to October 15 on a first-come, first-served basis. An Adventure Pass is required for overnighting in the Coon Creek area. No Adventure Pass is required when paying the regular campground fee at Heart Bar.

**FACILITIES:** Restrooms, picnic area, and camping.

**CONTACT:** Mill Creek Ranger Station: 909-382-2882.

Coon Creek is a meandering mountain creek that drains a yellow pine forest and provides the closest vehicle access possible to the headwaters of the Santa Ana River. There are 19 dispersed "yellow post" or primitive (no hookups) campsites available along Forest Road 1N02, below its crossing of the Pacific Crest Trail. These are free of charge, but they require an Adventure Pass.

Water is available along the road at the Heart Bar equestrian camp. Heart Bar has both an equestrian group camp and 94 standard Forest Service campsites that include handicap facilities, flush toilets, and water. There are no hookups. Family campground costs between $15 and $30, depending on vehicle size and season. Despite the high number of sites here, they provide adequate space for privacy, though crowds are possible on some summer weekends.

# South Fork Campground and Trailheads

**HIGHLIGHTS:** Camping so close to the river makes the South Fork Campground a highlight of any trip to the upper watershed.

**ACCESS:** South Fork Campground is 23 miles north of the Mill Creek Ranger Station on Hwy. 38.

**SEASON & HOURS:** The campground is open from May 15 to September 6 and costs $15 per site and $5 for each additional vehicle. The trailhead is open all year.

**FACILITIES:** Restrooms, picnic area, and camping.

**CONTACT:** Mill Creek Ranger Station: 909-382-2882. In summer, contact the Barton Flats Visitor Center: 909-794-4861.

South Fork Campground is the closest campground to the Santa Ana River in the San Bernardino Mountains. The South Fork flows along the northeastern edge of the campground and provides acoustics to go with the scenery. The flora here transitions from tall pines to stubby willows as you move from the actual campsites toward the river, which is narrow and fast along this stretch. Due to the dense vegetation along the edges, there are some good fishing spots.

The campground is one of the best in the forest for families because of its convenient location just off the highway and its proximity to other facilities such as the forest amphitheater. There are 24 sites, 17 of which include vehicle parking up to 25 feet, and there are seven tent-only sites with remote parking. A dump station and flush toilets are available at the site, but there are no hookups. Grayback Amphitheater, less than a half mile south on Hwy. 38 (on the opposite side of the road from the campground), hosts weekly interpretive campfire programs all summer. Check with the Barton Flats Visitor Center or Mill Creek Ranger Station for a schedule.

Just outside the campground, there are several places to access the Santa Ana River Trail. Immediately across Hwy. 38 from the campground is a trailhead where you can head up- or downstream. Heading downstream, hikers, mountain bikers, and equestrians can take the Santa Ana River Trail and travel 30 miles to the forest boundary below Morton Peak and just above Seven Oaks Dam. Though the trail officially ends at Morton Peak, there is a remnant unmaintained trail that

**Fork in the trail below Hwy. 38: Head up to the road, or down to the river.**

continues to Greenspot Road just beyond the Seven Oaks Dam. If you hike upstream, you will reach the junction with the South Fork Trail after 4 miles, and after 7 miles, you'll reach the Pacific Crest Trail.

To access the South Fork Trailhead for hikes into the San Gorgonio Wilderness, follow Hwy. 38 for 2 miles north of Barton Flats Visitor Center and turn right on Jenks Lake Road. Follow Jenks Lake Road for approximately 3 miles to the South Fork Trailhead.

# Barton Flats Visitor Center

**HIGHLIGHTS:** This is a great place to stop for the stories from longtime volunteer staff as well as to get current trail conditions.

**ACCESS:** The visitor center is located on Hwy. 38, approximately 6 miles north of Angelus Oaks and 20 miles north of the Mill Creek Ranger Station.

**SEASON & HOURS:** Open from mid-May to the first weekend in September.

**FACILITIES:** Restroom, picnic table, and interpretive displays.

**CONTACT:** Barton Flats Visitor Center: 909-794-4861.

Although it's small, the Barton Flats Visitor Center provides quality, up-to-date information on campgrounds, trail conditions, and weather for the San Gorgonio Wilderness Area and the Santa Ana River Canyon. The center is staffed all summer by volunteers—many of whom have long track records in the mountains and can answer most any query about local plants, animals, and geography. When the Mill Creek Ranger Station is busy, the Barton Flats Visitor Center is an alternative location for getting an Adventure Pass, wilderness permit, or other necessary information.

**Barton Flats Visitor Center packs a lot of information into a small space.**

# Santa Ana River Interpretive Site

**HIGHLIGHTS:** This site has easy access for even a standard passenger car (in summer), but it maintains a backcountry feel despite nearby residences.

**ACCESS:** This site is located on Seven Oaks Road (Forest Road 1N45) a half mile upstream (east) of Glass Road and 5 miles from Hwy. 38 on the Santa Ana River Trail.

**SEASON & HOURS:** Open all year, but the road may not be in good shape during the winter.

**FACILITIES:** Interpretive displays.

**CONTACT:** Mill Creek Ranger Station: 909-382-2882.

The Santa Ana River Interpretive Site is a 1-acre area with a short, stone-lined interpretive trail that documents the ecology and conservation of the upper Santa Ana River and its watershed. Additional interpretive displays dot the area, making this a great place to explore the river with the whole family. There is excellent access to the water here, and the site is great for picnics, fishing, and just soaking your feet in the rushing river.

Mature alders line the stream and are joined here and there by the occasional willow. No more than 10 yards from the river are patches of sagebrush, buckwheat, and rabbit brush. Bunchgrasses, golden yarrow, and coyote mint cover the ground, providing texture and color to the meadow-like spaces.

The Forest Service prohibits camping directly on the river, but those wishing to camp close to the river can do so at one of the many private resort camps located nearby and described on page 72. If you prefer more remote camping opportunities in the area, check with the Mill Creek Ranger Station (909-382-2882).

# Seven Oaks Village and Resort Cabins

**HIGHLIGHTS:** Quality fishing holes and the best veggie burger in the mountains make Seven Oaks a great place to vacation or just stop by for the day.

**ACCESS:** Resorts are located between 39000 and 41000 Seven Oaks Road. From Hwy. 38, head northwest on Glass Road for 2 miles to Seven Oaks Road and turn left.

**SEASON & HOURS:** Most resorts are open all year with reduced service in winter.

**FACILITIES:** Picnic area, store, camping, cabin rentals, and restaurant.

**CONTACT:** Mill Creek Ranger Station: 909-382-2882. Seven Oaks Lodge Camping and RV Park: 909-794-2917. Seven Oaks Mountain Cabins: 909-794-1277; www.sevenoaksmtcabins.com.

Along Seven Oaks Road, which loosely follows the Santa Ana River, there are numerous pullouts for easy river access and prized fishing. There are also several resorts, collectively known as the Seven Oaks Village, which offer cabin rentals, private group camps, pools, and more. The resorts include the Seven Oaks Lodge and Seven Oaks Mountain Cabins, which offer river access and opportunities for relaxation.

Rarely more than 20 feet wide and lined by tall trees and grasses, the river here has remained unchanged for a century or more. It is typical of high-country streams—fast moving, icy-green, and cold all year. Scattered pools form in front of fallen trees and around boulders. This is where prize trout hide and the brave and hardy swim. Alders, willows, cottonwoods, and the occasional sycamore or oak tree line the banks. Jeffrey and ponderosa pine are common in this area of yellow pine forest, and mugwort, poison oak, and grasses form the understory in this high-elevation riparian ribbon. Great Basin sagebrush and common buckwheat are common farther away from the active channel.

The Santa Ana River Trail crisscrosses the area but stays above the river here. Access the trail downstream of the resort below the village of Angeles Oaks off of Glass Road. Please be respectful of the many private residences in this area, including the Weesha Club.

# Thomas Hunting Grounds

**HIGHLIGHTS:** This is the most remote and primitive car camping in the watershed.

**ACCESS:** From the Mill Creek Ranger Station, take Hwy. 38 approximately 10 miles north to Forest Road 1N12 just before the town of Angelus Oaks. Turn left on 1N12 and continue for approximately 4 miles to the camping area. The camp is about halfway between Angelus Oaks and Morton Peak.

**SEASON & HOURS:** Camping is open all year on a first-come, first-served basis, but access may be limited due to weather conditions. An Adventure Pass is required for overnighting in this primitive area.

**FACILITIES:** Camping.

**CONTACT:** Mill Creek Ranger Station: 909-382-2882.

Thomas Hunting Grounds is an undeveloped, dispersed camping area popular with deer and turkey hunters from July to January. In the off season, it is an excellent location to stage hikes and mountain bike rides on the lower Santa Ana River Trail and to enjoy the San Bernardino Mountains without the summertime crowds at Barton Flats and Big Bear Lake.

**Backpacking above Thomas Hunting Grounds**

The area is a mix of conifer trees and chaparral. At just above 5000 feet in elevation, the area provides glimpses of the high peaks as well as a few vistas of the river wash and Inland Empire below.

The road here is rough and there are sometimes four-wheelers and motorcycles zooming down it. Though you can hear them coming, they may not see you, so stay aware.

## Oak Glen

Located a few miles off Interstate 10, northeast of the city of Yucaipa, at Yucaipa Blvd. in the San Bernardino Mountains, Oak Glen is famous for its apple farms, but it also provides visitors with the down-home atmosphere of a small mountain town.

Many of the apple growers also have stores where fresh-picked apples, apple juice, and apple pie can be purchased. A petting zoo, museum, historic area, and a variety of antique shops also attract visitors to Oak Glen.

Living history performances occur seasonally, so check with the chamber of commerce for show times. You might find yourself in the middle of an Old West shootout or Indian powwow.

One of the best stops for visitors with short itineraries is the historic Los Rios Rancho (909-797-1005; www.wildlandsconservancy.org), an old apple farm that is now operated by the Wildlands Conservancy, which also provides environmental education programs and hiking trails in the natural lands that border the rancho. Don't miss the famous apple cobbler or organic apple juice sold in the Los Rios Rancho store.

For more information about Oak Glen, visit the Apple Growers Association's website at www.oakglen.net.

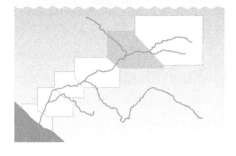

# SANTA ANA RIVER WASH AND UPPER INLAND EMPIRE

For most of its length, the Santa Ana River follows a wide, cobble-strewn bed that begins as the river escapes the confines of Seven Oaks Dam and enters what this guide refers to as Reach II. This stretch of river is also commonly called the Santa Ana River Wash because of its very wide and mostly dry bed. Beginning at the Seven Oaks Dam and extending downstream to Hwy. 60, the river here zigzags across a bed that can be as much as a mile wide but mostly is about a quarter mile in width.

Buckwheat, yucca, mulefat, and wild rose combine to cover the terraces, while the river itself meanders over medium cobble and between large boulders. A few cottonwoods dot the area, but there is no riparian "forest" to speak of. This is also home to the small but colorful plant called the Santa Ana River woolly star, a knee-high annual that is one of the many endangered species found in the watershed below the San Bernardino Mountains. Junipers also inhabit this area, adding to the strange mix of desert and riparian species that comprise the globally imperiled vegetation community known as alluvial sage scrub.

Unfortunately, access is limited in this area to a few short trails and on-street bike lanes. Much of this reach has been impacted by recreational and industrial misuse, but a cooperative planning effort between federal, state, and local governments will lead to a sustainable reserve that provides both ecological protection and recreational opportunities.

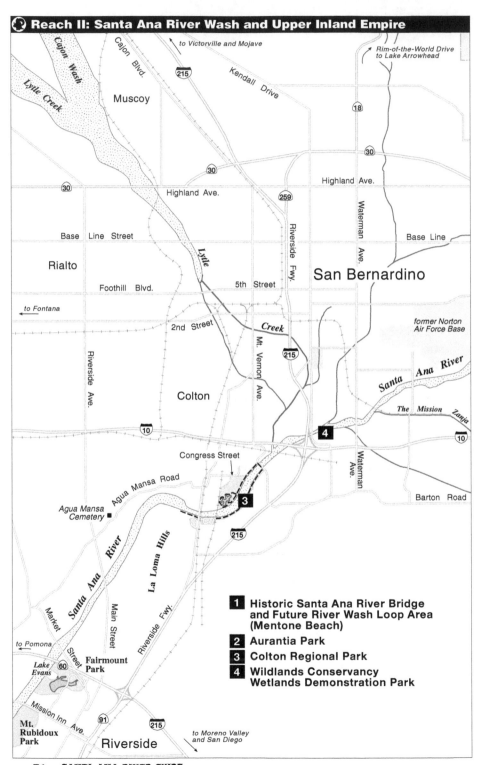

to Victorville and Mojave

Rim-of-the-World Drive
to Lake Arrowhead

Cajon Wash

Cajon Blvd.

215

Kendall Drive

Lytle Creek

Muscoy

18

30

30

30

Highland Ave.

Highland Ave.

259

Riverside Fwy.

Waterman Ave.

Base Line Street

Base Line

Lytle

Rialto

San Bernardino

Foothill Blvd.

5th Street

to Fontana

2nd Street

Creek

former Norton
Air Force Base

Mt. Vernon Ave.

215

Santa Ana River

Riverside Ave.

Colton

The Mission

Zanja

10

4

10

Congress Street

Waterman Ave.

Agua Mansa Road

Barton Road

Agua Mansa
Cemetery ■

3

215

Santa Ana River

La Loma Hills

to Pomona

Market Street

Main Street

Riverside Fwy.

**1** Historic Santa Ana River Bridge
and Future River Wash Loop Area
(Mentone Beach)

**2** Aurantia Park

**3** Colton Regional Park

**4** Wildlands Conservancy
Wetlands Demonstration Park

Lake
Evans

60

Fairmount
Park

Mt.
Rubidoux
Park

Mission Inn Ave.

91

215

to Moreno Valley
and San Diego

Riverside

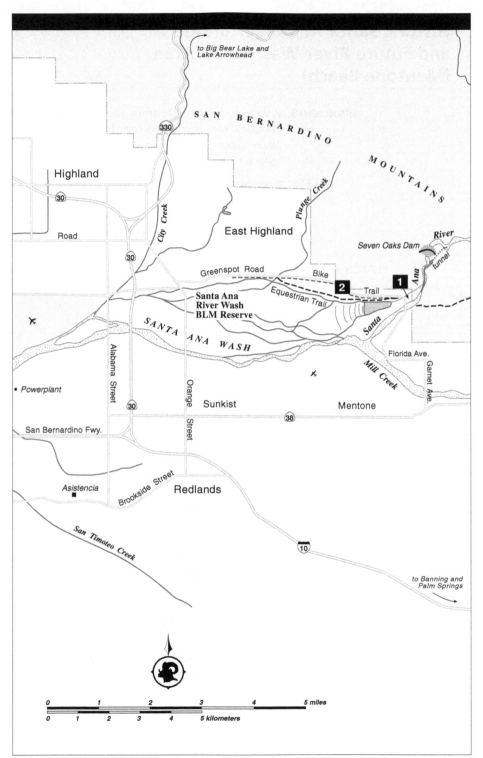

# Historic Santa Ana River Bridge
# and Future River Wash Loop Area
# (Mentone Beach)

**HIGHLIGHTS:** Known to locals as Mentone Beach, this area features cold, crisp water released from Seven Oaks Dam and relatively few people to share it with.

**ACCESS:** Greenspot Road between Church Street and Lugonia Ave. (Hwy. 38). Greenspot Road is the first official crossing of the Santa Ana River below the national forest and Seven Oaks Dam.

**SEASON & HOURS:** Future hours to be determined. Though officially discouraged, day use has been accepted from sunrise to sunset.

**FACILITIES:** Bike lane along Greenspot Road.

**CONTACT:** City of Highland: 909-864-6861; www.ci.highland.ca.us. San Bernardino Flood Control District: 909-794-7704; www.co.san-bernardino.ca.us/flood. Bureau of Land Management: 760-251-4800; www.blm.gov/ca/palmsprings/inland_empire.

Boulder-strewn and sun-bleached, this stretch marks the beginning of the river's journey across the floodplain. Until this point, the river is a fast-moving, tree-lined stream, but here the river opens into a wide, flat bed. Under normal conditions, the river braids its way through the Inland Empire, but depending on releases from Seven Oaks Dam, the river may be dry here.

There is no official park or reserve where Greenspot Road crosses the river, but the area is being planned as part of the Santa Ana River Wash Land Management and Habitat Conservation Plan, which encompasses 4365 acres of river and surrounding floodplain. This plan, along with recreational plans from the cities of Redlands and Highland and the county of San Bernardino, should result in an area useful to people as well as the animals and plants that have called this area home for eons. Today, this area is just widen open river bottom and floodplain terraces resembling the desert bajadas a few miles east but with some of the plants common at the coast.

The bridge that spans the river here was built in 1912 and will remain as part of the Santa Ana River Crest to Coast Trail, even after Greenspot Road is widened and a new bridge is constructed to the west of the existing one. There are also numerous pullouts along the road on the north side of the bridge, and there is much evidence that, even in autumn and winter, this area is a popular destination for the many people inhabiting the communities just a few miles away. Numerous trails wind from the roadside to the river's edge, but the only official trails in this reach are striped bike lanes along Greenspot Road and some horse and hiking trails that head south and west from Greenspot Road along Southern California Edison easements known locally as the Pole Road. The locals call this area Mentone Beach and cool themselves by frolicking in the cold waters that tumble from Seven Oaks Dam and sun themselves on the shore of the river.

Don't forget your hat and sunscreen. There is very little shade here except under the bridge and an occasional tree. Alluvial sage scrub covers most of the river terrace in this area. The river bottom is nearly

**Historic bridge below Seven Oaks Dam**

plantless except for several scattered willows and cottonwoods and, just below the historic bridge, a few tamarisk trees have managed to take root. Numerous stunted junipers grow throughout the wash, but their low growth structure and stiff limbs should not be counted on to provide much relief from the sun in summer or fall when temperatures regularly top 100°F.

Citrus farming and bee-keeping are still commonplace at the river canyon's mouth. Groves of citrus fruit line Greenspot Road on both sides of the river, and dozens of bee boxes are held behind locked pipe gates.

# Aurantia Park

**HIGHLIGHTS:** Aurantia Park is a well-designed park with quality features, clean restrooms, and plenty of parking.

**ACCESS:** 29700 Greenspot Road in Highland.

**SEASON & HOURS:** Open from dawn to dusk all year.

**FACILITIES:** Restrooms, interpretive displays, playground, trails, and a dog park.

**CONTACT:** City of Highland: 909-864-6861; www.ci.highland.ca.us.

Twelve-acre Aurantia Park, which is Highland's first dedicated open space, differs dramatically from the wild country still visible above it. Aurantia means "golden" and refers to the oranges that grow here. The land was donated to preserve the citrus heritage of the city of Highland, and also to preserve and showcase the native flora and fauna of the area, including yucca, buckwheat, and sages.

**Gateway to Aurantia Park**

The park serves both goals well, with large areas left natural and a citrus grove lining the back of the park. Aurantia Park remains almost hidden from passers-by as they speed down the road, and it would probably be completely missed if not for the attractive sign on stone columns at the roadside.

The park contains several trails for hiking and horseback riding. A historic bridge segment, once crossing the Santa Ana River and Plunge Creek, now crosses a small drainage that flows through the park. Even the hounds have claimed a section of this park, which has been set aside as a dog park.

Clean restrooms and parking make this a good staging area for explorations along the river. An equestrian trail crosses Greenspot Road less than a quarter mile west of the park and leads to the river.

# Colton Regional Park

**HIGHLIGHTS:** Colton Regional Park will be the first new regional park in the county in more than 25 years.

**ACCESS:** To be located at the northern edge of the city of Colton, on Congress Street, where the road meets the river.

**SEASON & HOURS:** Sunrise to 10 PM and camping when the park opens in 2008.

**FACILITIES:** When complete, the park will have restrooms, interpretive displays, trails, camping, and sports fields.

**CONTACT:** San Bernardino County Parks: 909-387-2591; www.co.san-bernardino.ca.us/parks.

When complete sometime between 2008 and 2010, Colton Regional Park will be a 150-acre oasis featuring sports fields, a lake, native habitat, a campground, and more. The first regional park in San Bernardino County in 25 years and the largest developed open space in Colton, the park will provide needed resources to many people.

Approximately 25 acres will be groomed into soccer, baseball, and multiuse fields. Picnic shelters will be constructed around manicured lawns providing for family events. A lake will be carved from the landscape, allowing fishing on nearly 15 acres of water. A campground will be developed to serve RV and tent campers.

Wildlife also will be served by this new park, which will include extensive planting of native habitat along the river. An additional 30-acre ecological reserve will be restored to include wetlands and other important vegetation communities. An environmental education center will be built to house exhibits and conduct educational programs for students and visitors.

The park is a unique project for which the county of San Bernardino, the city of Colton, and the Wildlands Conservancy have worked together to acquire and develop the land. San Bernardino County Parks will manage and maintain the facility when it's complete.

# Wildlands Conservancy Wetlands Demonstration Park

**HIGHLIGHTS:** Here you can find an inspiring pocket of wild in the middle of the city.

**ACCESS:** The wetlands are two blocks north of Interstate 10 next to the San Bernardino County Hall of Records at 222 Hospitality Lane in San Bernardino.

**SEASON & HOURS:** Sunrise to sunset.

**FACILITIES:** Interpretive displays and picnic tables will be complete by 2008.

**CONTACT:** The Wildlands Conservancy: 909-797-8507; www.wildlandsconservancy.org.

Tucked between the San Bernardino County Hall of Records and other commercial buildings, this 4-acre depression in the landscape will be transformed into an urban oasis by the Wildlands Conservancy, which is restoring native vegetation, creating new trails, and more. Plans for the area include additional habitat restoration, a boardwalk-style trail, and interpretive displays. Educational programs to serve the several nearby elementary schools will become a staple at this site, and a restaurant and entertainment facility that will look out onto the wetlands and river are planned for nearby.

Currently, this is a great place for bird-watching and is popular with locals on lunch and work breaks who come to enjoy Southern California black walnuts, willows, and mulefat. The Santa Ana River Bikeway also passes nearby, making this location an excellent stopover or staging area for rides on the river.

**The Wildlands Conservancy Wetlands Demonstration Park puts the "wild" in the city.**

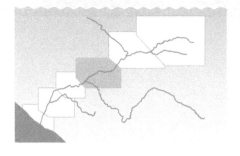

# SANTA ANA RIVER REGIONAL PARK AND LOWER INLAND EMPIRE: HIGHWAY 60 TO PRADO DAM

At Hwy. 60, the Santa Ana River begins to reclaim itself, leaving the restrictions of the channel it flows through in parts of San Bernardino and Colton. The wide riverbed is crisscrossed by a braided channel that forms wildlife habitat. Species include migratory songbirds, raptors, non-native wild pigs, and the protected Delhi sands flower loving fly. This is also a good place to find such rare species as legless lizards.

Riparian forest with mature Fremont cottonwood and arroyo willows lines much of this reach. Wild grape, blackberries, and pipestem clematis grow here, making some of the riverside forest impassible.

This reach has more preserved open space than any other stretch of river equal in length, except perhaps the mountain reach. Riverside County's Santa Ana River Regional Park complex comprises much of the open space; however, every city along the river and San Bernardino County contribute additional parks and reserves.

There are some gaps in the trail system here, though plans are underway to connect the river from Fairmount Park to Prado Dam by 2008. With the extensive trails, parks, and nature reserves, Reach III provides endless opportunities to explore one of the nicest stretches of the Santa Ana River.

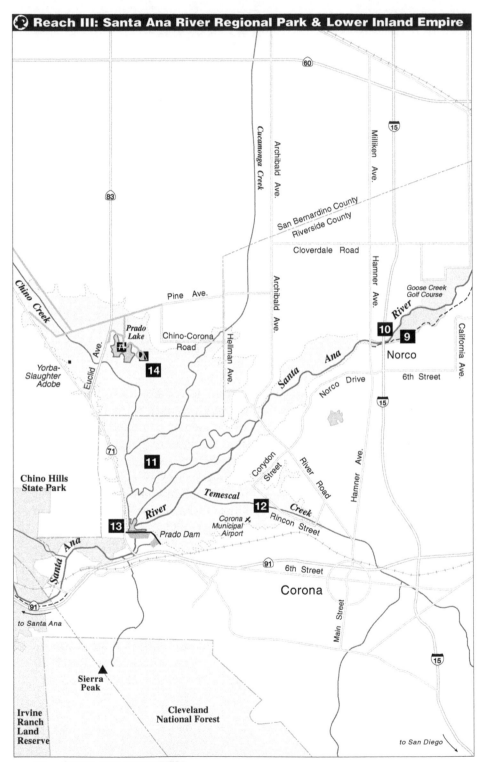

60

15

Cucamonga Creek

Archibald Ave.

Milliken Ave.

83

San Bernardino County
Riverside County

Cloverdale   Road

Hamner Ave.

Goose Creek
Golf Course

River

Pine   Ave.

Chino Creek

Archibald Ave.

**Prado
Lake**

Chino-Corona
Road

Hellman Ave.

**10**

**9**

California Ave.

Yorba-
Slaughter
Adobe

Euclid   Ave.

**14**

Santa   Ana

Norco

6th   Street

Norco   Drive

15

71

**11**

Corydon   Street

River   Road

Hamner   Ave.

**Chino Hills
State Park**

Temescal

**12**

Creek

Rincon   Street

**13**

River

Santa   Ana

Corona ✈
Municipal
Airport

Prado Dam

91

6th   Street

**Corona**

Main   Street

91

to Santa Ana

15

▲
Sierra
Peak

**Cleveland
National Forest**

**Irvine
Ranch
Land
Reserve**

to San Diego ↘

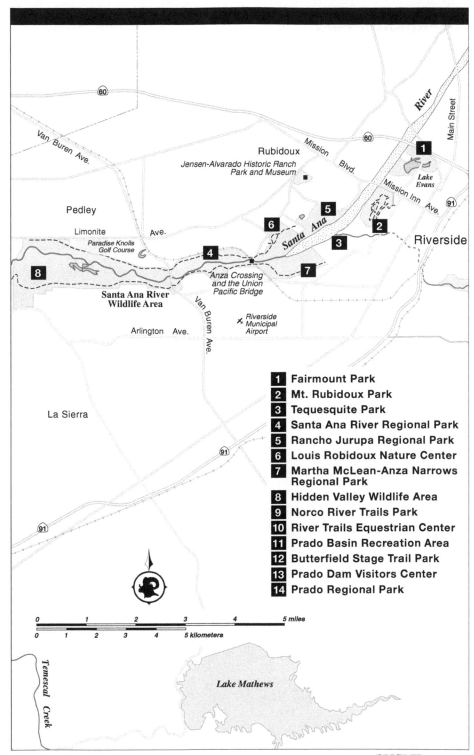

1  Fairmount Park
2  Mt. Rubidoux Park
3  Tequesquite Park
4  Santa Ana River Regional Park
5  Rancho Jurupa Regional Park
6  Louis Robidoux Nature Center
7  Martha McLean-Anza Narrows Regional Park
8  Hidden Valley Wildlife Area
9  Norco River Trails Park
10 River Trails Equestrian Center
11 Prado Basin Recreation Area
12 Butterfield Stage Trail Park
13 Prado Dam Visitors Center
14 Prado Regional Park

0    1    2    3    4    5 miles
0  1  2  3  4  5 kilometers

# Fairmount Park

**HIGHLIGHTS:** Lake Evans and the historic boathouse are great settings for picnics and group gatherings, while the willow thickets along the river are perfect for quick hikes and exploration.

**ACCESS:** 2601 Fairmount Blvd., Riverside.

**SEASON & HOURS:** 7 AM to 9 PM.

**FACILITIES:** Restrooms, playgrounds, picnic area, horseshoe pits, lake, tennis courts, bowling greens, and a golf course.

**CONTACT:** City of Riverside Parks Department: 951-826-2000; www.riversideca.gov/park_rec.

At 165 acres, Fairmount is a large urban park that serves Riverside in the same way Golden Gate Park and Central Park serve San Francisco and New York. In fact, Fairmount Park was designed by Central Park creator Frederick Law Olmstead, the father of American landscape architecture, who also designed the US Capitol Grounds and many other parks and communities throughout the country.

**The classic Lake Evans boathouse at Fairmount Park**

Typical of Olmstead's designs, Fairmount Park and the surrounding neighborhoods blend in and out of each other seamlessly, making Fairmount the literal backyard of many of the homes that border the park. Roads through the park meander, hugging the landscape rather than slicing across it. This design makes even a casual bike ride through the park a bit challenging, especially on the south end of the park.

The 25-acre Lake Evans spreads over the center of the park and is one of the main attractions. Pedal boats can be rented on weekends and fishing is popular from piers that extend over deeper areas of the lake to assist anglers in landing the prized catch. The lake is stocked with trout, catfish, and bass, and fishing here requires a state fishing license, which can be purchased at most sporting goods stores.

Many organized activities occur at Fairmount Park, including horseshoes and lawn bowling. The Isaac Walton League and the American Legion both have posts here, and the Fairmount Golf Course adds to the sporting opportunities and significantly increases the open space of the area.

The riparian forest and wetlands that line the Santa Ana River in this area also form the southwest boundary of Fairmount Park. Numerous foot trails lead from the park to the river (about a quarter mile away), but none is official or direct. Finding the river using these trails requires patience and a willingness to explore. Return visitors will find a favorite route they can call their own. If you want a simpler route to the river, follow the paved bike trail southwest from the southern edge of the park.

# Mt. Rubidoux Park

**HIGHLIGHTS:** The view from the top of Mt. Rubidoux, especially on a clear day, makes the strenuous climb to the top worth every breath.

**ACCESS:** 4706 Mt. Rubidoux Street, Riverside.

**SEASON & HOURS:** Sunrise to sunset.

**FACILITIES:** Interpretive displays and trails.

**CONTACT:** City of Riverside Parks Department: 951-826-2000; www.riversideca.gov/park_rec.

In the early 1900s, Frank Miller, who originally owned the Mission Inn, purchased 1337-foot Mt. Rubidoux from the Louis Rubidoux Ranch, using money from railroad magnate Henry Huntington. Miller, who wanted to develop custom home sites in the area, turned Mt. Rubidoux over to the city in 1906 to build a park, in the hopes that an attractive park nearby would help sell the lots. A road was cut to the top and dozens of California pepper trees were planted along it. The park was immediately popular, but the community that Miller envisioned was never developed on the mountain. However, over the next several decades, many custom homes were constructed in the area.

A cross was erected on top of the mountain to memorialize Father Junipero Serra, founder of the California missions, and in 1909, the first documented outdoor Easter service in the country was held on the site.

**The peace tower in Mt. Rubidoux Park stands vigil over Riverside.**

The service proved popular and continues today. Later in the century, a peace tower was erected on the site, and the tall stone and brick tower still stands vigil over the town of Riverside.

Today, the park occupies nearly 150 acres and provides visitors with astounding views of the city of Riverside and part of the Santa Ana River watershed. The park is sparsely vegetated, or so it feels if you climb the road anytime between July and October. Low-growing grasses, mostly non-native, cover much of the site and dry out early in the season. In most years, the site is green from December to March, but it is always dependent on rainfall. Regardless of the season or color of the landscape, great views are always guaranteed from the peak of Mt. Rubidoux, especially on warm, windy fall days or cold winter ones. In addition to views down to the Santa Ana River, the peaks of San Gorgonio, Mt. Baldy, and Saddleback are visible, as is much of San Diego County. Stone seating areas have been constructed on top of the mountain and at the foot of the cross and tower, making the climb much like a pilgrimage.

Mt. Rubidoux is a pedestrian-oriented park and motorized vehicles are strictly prohibited. The site makes a great location for quick workouts or extended causal ascents to the peak.

## Mission Inn

Originally opened as a 12-room, two-story adobe in 1876, Riverside's historic Mission Inn (3649 Mission Inn Ave.; 951-784-0300; www.missioninn.com) now boasts 239 rooms and 28 suites, and it covers an entire city block. Each new wing in the hotel also added a new twist or style. Known as Riverside's grand hotel, this establishment has hosted many dignitaries, royalty, and even President Teddy Roosevelt.

Because its popularity was dropping continually after the 1930s, the hotel changed ownership several times. Eventually, it fell into disrepair and closed its doors. It became the city's property in 1985.

As part of Riverside's revitalization efforts, the hotel underwent a complete restoration and reopened in 1992 under new private ownership. Today, the hotel is a popular stop for many traveling to Riverside and also for locals seeking a quality meal or just wanting to enjoy the atmosphere.

The Mission Inn Foundation offers daily tours of the hotel, and special arrangements for group tours can be made by calling ahead.

# Tequesquite Park

**HIGHLIGHTS:** Watch red-tailed hawks hunt in the tall grasses that carpet this future park site.

**ACCESS:** 4825 Tequesquite Ave, Riverside.

**SEASON & HOURS:** Although the area has not yet been officially developed or opened as a park, day use of the area has been accepted by authorities.

**FACILITIES:** Trails.

**CONTACT:** City of Riverside Parks Department: 951-826-2000; www.riversideca.gov/park_rec.

At the time of this writing, Tequesquite Park was little more than a large urban vacant lot. However, it provides one of the best opportunities for a new city park along the Santa Ana River upstream of the Prado Basin, and it already has an extensive trail system, some roadside parking, and great access to the river. Tequesquite provides habitat for many species of urban wildlife and some not often associated with human habitation, like the occasional marsh hawk or bobcat.

The park site is mostly level and connects to the Santa Ana River near the old landfill, which is also undeveloped and easily could be converted for recreational uses. In 2004, a Riverside Blue Ribbon Task Force that focused on the Santa Ana River suggested that both locations be developed into traditional urban parks with playing fields and a system of trails that connect to the river and other open-space areas. Although a timeline has not been set, the city has acquired the land and is planning to develop parks on the sites soon. Many trail and park advocates look forward to the day when these areas are permanently developed into recreational open space.

**Palms tower over willow at the future Tequesquite Park site.**

# Santa Ana River Regional Park

**HIGHLIGHTS:** Discover a "wild" Santa Ana River in the middle of the city.

**ACCESS:** Santa Ana River Regional Park has many access points between Interstate 15 and Van Buren Ave. See a map for specific locations.

**SEASON & HOURS:** Sunrise to sunset.

**FACILITIES:** Restrooms, picnic areas, and equestrian staging area.

**CONTACT:** Riverside County Regional Parks and Open-Space District: 951-955-4310; www.riversidecountyparks.org.

Santa Ana River Regional Park is the generic name given to the thousands of natural, open-space acres that line the river throughout Riverside County. Specific locations through much of the park have their own names, such as Louis Robidoux Nature Center (page 97) and Hidden Valley Wildlife Area (page 99), which are described later in this section.

**Santa Ana River Regional Park rests between snow and surf.**

A classic river scene at Santa Ana River Regional Park

Two things bind all of this land together. The first is the river, which laces through and around the various parcels of wilderness. The second binding element is that all of these lands are managed by Riverside County Regional Parks and Open-Space District—a unique arrangement because the district does not own all of the land. They lease or contract manage much of it.

Santa Ana River Regional Park maintains the appearance and function the Santa Ana River has had for centuries, and therefore much of the natural and wild diversity of the river is evident here. Due to many past management actions, the Riverside County Regional Parks and Open-Space District now has to take many restorative steps such as removing non-native invasive plants and enhancing stream banks. The regional park has miles of trails for hikers, bikers, and equestrians. The nature of the land also provides many bluff-top overlooks, making the park a great place to go to see the river and its surroundings.

# Rancho Jurupa Regional Park

**HIGHLIGHTS:** Rancho Jurupa provides a diversity of wildlife-watching opportunities, especially around the lake and at the river. Keep your eyes open for the numerous kingfishers that hunt in this area. Legless lizards are also found here.

**ACCESS:** 4800 Crestmore Road, Riverside.

**SEASON & HOURS:** 7 AM to sunset.

**FACILITIES:** Restrooms (with showers), playgrounds, picnic area, camping, stocked fishing lakes, horseshoe pits, and a nature center.

**CONTACT:** Riverside County Regional Parks and Open-Space District: 951-684-7032; www.riversidecountyparks.org.

Rancho Jurupa Park, a 350-acre Riverside County Regional Park on the edge of Riverside, was named for the Spanish-era rancho that once occupied these lands. Today, the park maintains a historic feel over much of its acreage, and it includes an historic building that now houses the Riverside County Regional Parks and Open-Space District headquarters. A dense riparian jungle connects the park to the Santa Ana River.

The park will see major improvements in the next few years, including the addition of a miniature golf course and a water park, slated for completion by 2008. These modernizations are not necessary to have a memorable experience at Rancho Jurupa Regional Park, but they will add recreational opportunities to the area.

Currently, the park is already home to two lakes. The lake that is farther south is surrounded by cattails and other wetland species and appears natural. Waterfowl are common in this lake, but you must look closely because they tend to hide in the dense foliage along the shore. The other lake, located north of the parking area, is newer and is maintained for fishing, with better access from its shoreline. Anglers are welcome to cast their lines in either lake.

Trails lead from the park to the Santa Ana River, where the riparian forest is dense, webbed with wild grape, and bordered by numerous marshy areas. The trails pass private property and visitors are expected

**The "old pond" at Rancho Jurupa**

to respect the boundaries. Many equestrians use the area, so please yield to horses.

The park has nearly 100 campsites that range from full-hookup RV spots to primitive locations with only a fire ring provided for overnight guests. Showers are available at the campground for an additional fee.

Much of the park is grass and passive open space, making Rancho Jurupa a great place for a picnics or a quick escape from the city. Picnic tables, horseshoe pits, and playgrounds are dispersed throughout the park.

# Louis Robidoux Nature Center

**HIGHLIGHTS:** Many activities are available here, but perhaps the best one is a hike on the Willow Creek Trail and trying your luck at finding all 33 critters hiding in the panoramic mural inside the nature center.

**ACCESS:** 5370 Riverview Lane, Riverside.

**SEASON & HOURS:** Open Saturdays, 10 AM to 4 PM, and weekdays by reservation.

**FACILITIES:** Restrooms, interpretive displays, picnic area, and equestrian facilities.

**CONTACT:** Louis Robidoux Nature Center: 951-683-4880; www.riversidecountyparks.org.

Part of the Santa Ana River Regional Park, the Louis Robidoux Nature Center is a quaint facility nestled between pecan groves on the banks of Willow Creek at its confluence with the Santa Ana River. Don't let the typical urban-park-style building discourage you. What it lacks in outside character, the facility makes up for inside, with panoramic exhibits of the Santa Ana River watershed, live animals, and a wealth of information on local natural history. The staff is very helpful and friendly, and some have been around long enough to impart a great deal of Santa Ana River experience.

The nature center grounds blend seamlessly with the rest of the park. From the center, you can follow the Willow Creek Trail through a dense, closed-canopy, willow-cottonwood forest to the banks of the Santa Ana. Be sure to bring your binoculars, as several wetland areas along the path shelter red-winged black birds, and the mature cottonwoods are home to red-tailed hawks. Thickets of wild grape line the trail, and elderberry bushes are thick with fruit in early summer. You can also follow a self-guided interpretive trail using a trail guide from the center.

# Martha McLean-Anza Narrows Regional Park

**HIGHLIGHTS:** Views of the river and historic Union Pacific Railroad Bridge should get you into this park, while the casual atmosphere and quiet setting will keep you coming back.

**ACCESS:** 5759 Jurupa Ave., Riverside.

**SEASON & HOURS:** 7 AM to sunset.

**FACILITIES:** Restrooms, picnic area, and trails.

**CONTACT:** Riverside County Regional Parks and Open-Space District: 951-683-1653; www.riversidecountyparks.org.

Forty-acre Martha McLean-Anza Narrows Regional Park sits atop a shady bluff with sweeping views of the river. The rolling landscape, which includes a mix of shaded picnic areas and open turf, terminates at the bluffs that drop steeply to the river. Dense, riparian woodland marks the foot of the bluff, but river access is limited due to the soft, easily eroded and nearly vertical cliffs that separate the park from the river.

A plaque in the southwest corner of the park marks the point at which the Anza Party crossed the river in 1774 and again in 1776. This spot also provides excellent views of the historic and architecturally stunning Union Pacific Railroad Bridge. The Santa Ana River Bikeway can be accessed at this location.

**A shady site at Martha McLean-Anza Narrows Regional Park**

# Hidden Valley Wildlife Area

**HIGHLIGHTS:** Views from the south bluff and nature center, great birding, and big, juicy mulberries make Hidden Valley worth the visit.

**ACCESS:** 11401 Arlington Ave., Riverside. Hidden Valley also can be accessed from Santa Ana River Regional Park on the north shore of the river off of Limonite Drive.

**SEASON & HOURS:** The nature center is open Saturdays, 10 AM to 4 PM, and weekdays by reservation.

**FACILITIES:** Restrooms, trails, nature center, and an equestrian staging area.

**CONTACT:** Hidden Valley Wildlife Area: 951-785-7452; www.riversidecountyparks.org.

Hidden Valley Wildlife Area is a 1500-acre reserve stretching along nearly 5 miles of the Santa Ana River between Riverside and Norco. It is a densely vegetated area covered with poison hemlock, mulefat, and other shrubs on lower hillsides and benches above the river. The bottomlands are home to mature riparian woodlands, which include cottonwoods, willows, alders, and sycamores. Several ponds and marshlands also are located in the reserve. The higher bluffs and hillsides surrounding the reserve are mostly non-native grassland.

**Looking downstream at Hidden Valley**

**A view of the headwaters from Hidden Valley Nature Center**

More than 25 miles of hiking and equestrian trails traverse the reserve, providing access to the river and great views from the bluffs. Several parking areas, including equestrian staging areas, are available from the main entrance to the reserve.

The entire reach of the river provides great opportunities for wildlife watching, with opportunities to see yellow-breasted chats, orioles, western blue birds, and half a dozen red-tailed hawks—sometimes in less than one hour. Wild pigs still haunt the thickets here, although there is an effort to eliminate them from the rich, ecological area.

Although this area is often lumped together with the Santa Ana River Regional Park, it is actually a separate facility. Hidden Valley is owned by California Department of Fish and Game, but it is managed by the Riverside County Regional Parks and Open-Space District.

# Norco River Trails Park

**HIGHLIGHTS:** The wild and seemingly untamed river and its riparian jungle make River Trails a great place to visit whether on foot or horseback.

**ACCESS:** 4545 Hamner Ave., Norco.

**SEASON & HOURS:** Sunrise to sunset.

**FACILITIES:** Trails.

**CONTACT:** Norco Parks and Recreation: 951-270-5632; www.norco.ca.us/depts./parks_rec.

The name says it all: Norco River Trails Park is nothing more than 277 acres of river-bottom trails. There are no extra frills, just you, the river, and plenty of room to wander. This area is a jungle of willow, cottonwood, mulefat, and other riparian plants intersected only by trails and river channels. Visitors are likely to encounter wildlife here, including egrets and herons, coyotes and fox, and maybe even a wild pig. Such rare or protected species as least bells vireo, Santa Ana suckers, and legless lizards also have been seen in the area.

There is no official parking for this area. Look for street parking along Hamner Ave. or check the lots at the River Trails Equestrian Center (page 102). The park is open to equestrians and pedestrians only. There currently is no bicycle access, but the Santa Ana River Bikeway should be complete through this area by 2007.

**The riparian jungle at Norco River Trails Park**

# River Trails Equestrian Center

**HIGHLIGHTS:** This is a great place to start a dayhike or horseback ride to access Norco River Trails Park.

**ACCESS:** 4545 Hamner Ave., Norco.

**SEASON & HOURS:** 8 AM to sunset.

**FACILITIES:** Restrooms and horse boarding, training, and rentals.

**CONTACT:** River Trails Equestrian Center: 951-736-9800.

Entering this dry, dust-covered, and shadeless facility is like stepping back in time to the Wild West. Herds of horses stare at visitors from behind peeling and sun-parched plank corrals, only moving to swat at flies with their tails. A couple donkeys also reside here. Bring your 10-gallon hat—this place gets hot!

Part boarding facility and part hourly rental facility, this stable is directly on the river and provides excellent access to miles of shoreline. Just beyond the stables is the mature willow woodland of Norco River Trails Park (page 101), which has plenty of shade and is a bird-watcher's paradise. Listen closely and you're likely to hear the call of an endangered least bells vireo or tropical song of a yellow breasted chat.

Horses rent for about $20 per hour or $40 for two hours, with the third hour free. Call ahead to check with the facility operator about trailoring in your own horse or for permission to park here for a hike. They have supported access in the past, but things can change, and this is private property.

# Prado Basin Recreation Area

**HIGHLIGHTS:** Watch things that fly, from vireos to Cessnas.

**ACCESS:** There are numerous access points for Prado Basin. At the time of this writing, there was much construction activity in the area. Call the Army Corps of Engineers (number below) for best access locations, hours, and appropriate activities.

**SEASON & HOURS:** Varies based on conditions, but generally day use only.

**FACILITIES:** Restrooms, trails, archery range, municipal airport, dog training, and hunting areas.

**CONTACT:** Army Corps of Engineers: 213-452-3908; www.recreation.gov/detail.cfm?ID=468.

Prado Basin Recreation Area provides a mix of recreational opportunities—from fishing and hunting to flying at a municipal airport—on 4823 acres of land that may be completely submerged in some years, or may go nearly a decade with no water closures at all. Dog training,

**The Prado Basin Recreation Area is vast.**

Photo by Bobby Palmer

skeet shooting, trail running, and bird-watching are just some of the many organized and casual activities that go on in the more than 1000 acres developed for recreation in Prado Basin. More than 3700 acres of the recreation area remain natural and undeveloped.

The landscape in the Prado Basin is as diverse as the activities that occur here. The Orange County Water District manages more than 300 acres of wetlands that treat Santa Ana River Water prior to its percolation into the groundwater basin downstream. Hundreds of acres of riparian forest are home to endangered least bells vireos, southwest willow flycatchers, and Santa Ana suckers. Even the Delhi sands flower loving fly sometimes can be found in the Prado Basin.

More than 11,500 acres of open space exist in the Prado Basin, and much of that can be accessed through the Prado Basin Recreation Area. Bring your binoculars, a hat, and sturdy shoes because there is plenty to see at this hot, rugged, and diverse recreational landscape.

# Butterfield Stage Trail Park

**HIGHLIGHTS:** Butterfield has the amenities of an urban park plus access to extensive wild areas.

**ACCESS:** 1900 West Butterfield Drive, Corona.

**SEASON & HOURS:** 5 AM to 10:30 PM.

**FACILITIES:** Restrooms, playgrounds, picnic area, dog park, and an exercise course.

**CONTACT:** Corona Parks and Recreation: 951-736-2241; www.ci.corona.ca.us/depts/parks.

Butterfield Stage Trail Park has an excellent mix of open space used for everything from ball fields and playgrounds to dense riparian forest. In fact, this 64-acre park is a great place for a quick break for those craving a walk on the wild side or some lunchtime birding. It is Corona's largest sports park.

The park is named for the historic Butterfield Stage Route that ran between St. Louis and San Francisco from 1858 through the 1860s. Memorialized in many places along its route, the stagecoach played an important role in bringing settlers from the East into Southern California. At the time, the Santa Ana River was an unpopular stretch for stage drivers because of the questionable terrain and the bandits who were believed to use the forest along the river for shelter before robbing passengers. The river was mostly dry, but sometimes it roared wide, deep, and strong, and quicksand was also an occasional concern for those crossing the river.

Today, the park is adjacent to Corona Municipal Airport and the Prado Basin Recreation Area. Balloons, model airplanes, and other airborne objects are strictly forbidden here. With the opportunity to watch the small private aircraft take off and land, the airport adds another element not present at many other parks.

# Prado Dam Visitors Center

**HIGHLIGHTS:** Learn the complexity of the Prado Dam operation—essential for anyone wanting to better understand the Santa Ana River.

**ACCESS:** 2493 Pomona-Rincon Road, Corona.

**SEASON & HOURS:** By reservation only.

**FACILITIES:** Restrooms and interpretive displays.

**CONTACT:** US Army Corps of Engineers: 951-898-6169.

The Prado Dam Visitors Center is an unassuming portable building on the edge of a major construction staging area. Huge trucks carrying cement, gravel, and other construction materials whiz by the parking area to and from the dam-construction site. Signs hang on the fences reminding all visitors that this is an Army Corps of Engineers project and a hardhat area. Cranes tower above the trees in the distance, and the warning alarms of heavy equipment moving replace the bird songs that Prado has become famous for. Although this may not be what most people expect from one of Southern California's most important eco-logical areas, it is an experience worth having.

Inside the building, which will be at this site at least until 2011, when the dam is complete, exhibits trace the history of the area over the past 5000 years. Visitors learn about past inhabitants including Native Americans, Californios, and the settlers of the town of Prado and Rin-con. Just as interesting are the interpretive displays of the Prado Dam and its past, present, and future. Highlighting this explanation are images of past flooding.

The Prado Dam effort, scheduled for completion in 2011, is part of the Santa Ana River Mainstem Project, which is aimed at providing flood control for the watershed. Often seen from the freeways that carve the edge of the basin, Prado is known for the patriotic mural that covers the spillway. After visiting the center, however, it's impossible to look at the project the same way. What seems like a mound of dirt and concrete is really an elaborate system of gates, channels, and controls worth a closer look and better understanding for everyone who lives downstream.

The visitor center is expected to remain open until the construction project is complete. Until then, this is the only way to access much of the Prado Basin around the dam.

# Prado Regional Park

**HIGHLIGHTS:** Prado Regional Park provides for an easy escape from the housing developments that have begun to creep into the Chino Basin.

**ACCESS:** 16700 South Euclid Ave., Chino.

**SEASON & HOURS:** 7 AM to 10 PM.

**FACILITIES:** Restrooms (with showers), picnic area, camping, and a store.

**CONTACT:** San Bernardino County Parks: 909-597-4260; www.co.san-bernardino.ca.us/parks/prado.htm.

This 2000-acre park, located in the heart of the Prado Basin, includes a lake, picnic sites, and campgrounds. Much of the park is covered with cool, green grass, though some shade is available under trees and picnic shelters.

Prado Regional Park provides a great escape from the rapidly developing neighborhoods of the Chino Hills, the Prado Basin, and rest of the Inland Empire, however, it should not be mistaken for a wilderness park. Prado Regional comes complete with a small grocery store, hot showers, a golf course, and boat rentals.

Fishing is encouraged at the lake, which is stocked with trout, catfish, and bass. Tournaments are held seasonally. If you don't fish, pedal boats are available for rent. The campgrounds range from nearly primitive tent sites with nearby water, to RV sites with full hookups. Twenty-five additional sites have water and electricity.

**The lake at Prado Regional Park**

*Photo by Matt Shook*

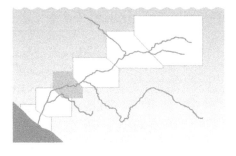

# SANTA ANA CANYON

The Santa Ana Canyon Reach of the river runs downstream from Prado Dam to the crossing of the 91 Freeway. To non-river folks, the "91 Freeway corridor" is one of the region's slowest-moving, literally crawling along the southern bank of the river for this entire reach. Most people driving this stretch probably don't know where the river starts or ends, but they might enjoy the view of trees, birds, and the occasional cyclist that breaks up the monotony of warehouses and strip malls that line most of the freeways in Southern California.

This is a transitional stretch of the river, as it begins in a wild and free-flowing setting and ends in a controlled, utilitarian environment. Gushing free of the Prado Dam, the river carves its way through Santa Ana Canyon just as it has for 12 million years. In fact, Santa Ana Canyon was formed as tectonic activity slowly formed the Santa Ana Mountains and the Chino Hills. Just as it has for eons, the river flow here repeatedly scours sediment, creating a narrow canyon and a gap between the hills and mountains. The river is narrow and deep and cuts a distinct channel through the canyon. Because of this formation, raft and canoe companies have begun to explore the canyon as a potential spot for commercially viable river trips. Proponents would like to make this the first water trail in Orange County.

As the river leaves the canyon and enters the Orange County floodplain, riprap-lined levies form boundaries to the channel, and the river becomes wide and shallow, except during heavy rain when it roars over check dams on its way to the ocean.

Here, the Santa Ana River Bikeway winds along the southern levy just below the freeway, but it remains secluded for about 3 miles, from Green River Drive to Gypsum Canyon. At Coal Canyon Road, there is access to the Cleveland National Forest and other natural open-space reserves that are described later in this chapter. At Gypsum Canyon, the trail leaves the south levy and crosses the river over the Gypsum Canyon Bridge before proceeding along the north levy to Imperial Hwy. The river remains wild and heavily vegetated to the Weir Canyon crossing.

At Weir Canyon, both the river and the trail become slightly more civilized. The river appears to widen, however, it likely is an illusion caused by the sudden absence of river-bottom vegetation. Check dams keep the river bottom flat and the water shallow. The trail also stays level from Weir Canyon Road to Imperial Hwy. Just before Imperial Hwy., a trestle-style bridge brings the trail back to the south, where it remains on that levy for about the next 5 miles.

At Imperial Hwy., the river enters a more utilitarian reach, and diversions for groundwater recharge begin. A second channel is developed north of the mainstem, and inflatable rubber dams divert half the river's flow into settling ponds and a new channel. The trail also becomes more urban here, with trailside landscaping consisting mostly of exotic trees and shrubs and carpeted with turf-like grass.

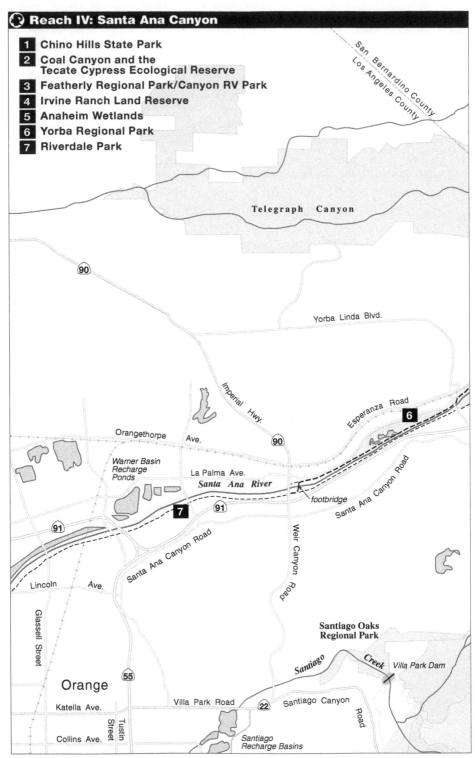

**1** Chino Hills State Park

**2** Coal Canyon and the
Tecate Cypress Ecological Reserve

**3** Featherly Regional Park/Canyon RV Park

**4** Irvine Ranch Land Reserve

**5** Anaheim Wetlands

**6** Yorba Regional Park

**7** Riverdale Park

San Bernardino County

Los Angeles County

Telegraph Canyon

90

Yorba Linda Blvd.

Imperial Hwy.

Esperanza Road

**6**

Orangethorpe Ave.

90

Warner Basin
Recharge
Ponds

La Palma Ave.

*Santa Ana River*

footbridge

Santa Ana Canyon Road

**7**

91

91

Santa Ana Canyon Road

Weir Canyon Road

Lincoln Ave.

Santiago Oaks
Regional Park

Glassell Street

*Santiago* Creek

Villa Park Dam

Orange

55

Katella Ave.

Villa Park Road

22

Santiago Canyon

Santiago Canyon Road

Tustin Street

Collins Ave.

Santiago
Recharge Basins

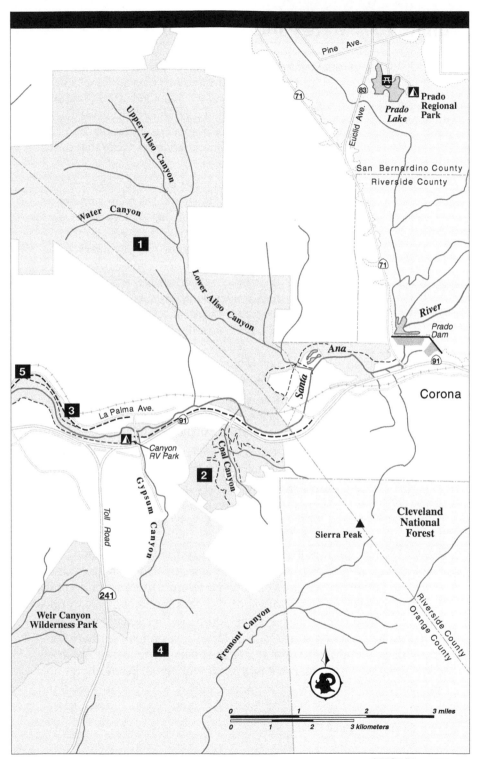

# Chino Hills State Park

This 12,452-acre park is a jewel, full of surprises hidden amongst its folded rolling hills. Mostly non-native grasses cover the slopes, but the occasional native needle grass can still be found. Park staff and volunteers are working to restore areas of the park so native grasses once again are dominant. Coastal sage scrub and chaparral-associated plants can be found on south-facing slopes and ridges. Southern California black walnuts provide shaded retreats on many of the trails above streams as well as trails with north-facing slopes. Canyon bottoms are home to willows, sycamores, and other riparian woodland species. Perhaps the most important resource provided by Chino Hills State Park is its role as a wildlife corridor connecting the Whittier-Puente Hills ecosystem to the Santa Ana Mountains, helping to ensure the survival of important wildlife species such as mountain lions.

With an elevation ranging from 450 to 1700 feet, Chino Hills State Park is popular with mountain bikers and trail runners, but it is also big enough for the quiet hiker seeking solitude. Equestrians can access the park from Carbon Canyon Road or from the main entrance to the park at Rolling M Ranch, where pipe corrals are available on a first-come, first-served basis.

The newest addition to the park includes much of Coal Canyon in Orange County and is the park's only acreage south of the Santa Ana River. This canyon was once the site of a proposed development that would have covered it with houses, but biologists in the 1980s and '90s found it to be the preferred crossing of mountain lions between the Santa Ana Mountains and the Chino Hills. Nearly $20 million was raised by private donations to purchase the land.

One major alteration, however, has occurred in the canyon. For the first time in California history, a freeway interchange was closed to benefit wildlife. High fences were constructed to direct lions and other critters under the freeway overpass and to keep them from attempting to cross traffic lanes.

The Coal Canyon section of park is most conveniently reached by taking the Santa Ana River Bikeway westbound from the entrance of Green River Golf Course. A small dirt parking area is located there and can accommodate 20 cars. From Coal Canyon, visitors can access the Cleveland National Forest, the Tecate Cypress Ecological Reserve, and the Irvine Ranch Land Reserve. In total, more than 200,000 acres of natural open space in the Santa Ana Mountains can be accessed from the Santa Ana River.

**Strolling the South Ridge Trail, Chino Hills State Park**

# Coal Canyon and the Tecate Cypress Ecological Reserve

**HIGHLIGHTS:** From here, you can look down over the Santa Ana Canyon and watch the next generation of tecate cypress grow. This is especially nice at sunrise as the new light reflects off of the river.

**ACCESS:** Upper Coal Canyon between Chino Hills State Park and the Cleveland National Forest. Access by foot, bike, or horseback via Coal Canyon Trail (see directions under Chino Hills State Park description, on page 112) or from Black Star Canyon.

**SEASON & HOURS:** By reservation only. Day use in Chino Hills State Park is $4.

**FACILITIES:** Trails.

**CONTACT:** California Department of Fish and Game: 858-467-4209; www.dfg.ca.gov/lands.

Coal Canyon and the Tecate Cypress Ecological Reserve are key parts of the Coal Canyon biological corridor, but it also protects the limited range of several species. In particular, the reserve is home to the planet's northernmost stand of tecate cypress. The tree's range stretches south from Coal Canyon to the Baja Peninsula.

The oldest and largest tecate cypress known once grew in this grove, but a fire destroyed the tree in 2003. In most situations, the loss of such a tree would be mourned, but not so with this species. Tecate cypress actually require fire to complete their reproductive process. Their thick, dense cones open only when burned. Therefore, this fire may prove to be an important event for the long-term health of the species in general and this grove in particular.

Other species benefiting from the protections granted in this reserve include the golden eagle, mountain lion, California spotted owl, and Mexican free-tailed bat. You can reach the reserve from the Main Divide Road in the Cleveland National Forest or hike to it from Chino Hills State Park via the Coal Canyon section of park.

# Featherly Regional Park/Canyon RV Park

**HIGHLIGHTS:** This park is an excellent choice for spur-of-the-moment overnighters who want to enjoy the river. The site will likely play a role in future rafting programs.

**ACCESS:** 24001 Santa Ana Canyon Road, Anaheim.

**SEASON & HOURS:** Year-round camping and very restricted day use is available in the campground area. Call the office for access information. The trails through the wilderness area are open to the public from sunrise to sunset. Camping fees range from $35 to $60 nightly.

**FACILITIES:** Restrooms (with showers), camping and other lodging, store, and swimming pool.

**CONTACT:** Canyon RV Park: 714-637-0210; www.canyonrvpark.com.

Featherly Regional Park, operated as Canyon RV Park by a private vendor, is located on 795 acres with 140 RV sites (full hookups), several tent sites, a dozen tent cabins, and 66 acres of developed land. Tent use is restricted to organized groups, and day use of the 66 acres of developed public land has been restricted to organized groups by the park management.

Unfortunately, non-RV users have given this park poor reviews in recent years, and the list of rules for those entering in RVs is long. Originally, it was a popular public park, but Orange County decided to experiment with private management following the municipal bankruptcy in the early 1990s. Many people within Orange County Harbors, Beaches, and Parks Department consider this experiment a failure.

The remaining 729 acres of wild land, which is not part of Canyon RV Park, can be accessed from the Santa Ana River Trail. This land is pure wilderness surrounding the Santa Ana River. Mature cottonwoods, sycamores, and willows shade the river and the miles of hiking and biking trails within the park. Although parking is limited, access to this area of the park can be made from La Palma Ave. without paying the park-entrance fee.

Canyon RV Park has made substantial improvements to the facilities at Featherly Regional Park, and the site now makes an excellent location for large group campouts and gatherings.

# Irvine Ranch Land Reserve

**HIGHLIGHTS:** Experience the rare opportunity to see Orange County the way the Tongva/Gabrielino did—before it was Orange County.

**ACCESS:** The Irvine Ranch once covered nearly a third of Orange County, and access to the reserve that remains open space today is spread out nearly as wide. There is limited access through Gypsum, Coal, and Weir canyons, as well as numerous locations along Santiago Canyon Road. Contact the reserve for appropriate access points, as these are changed periodically to reduce impacts on the land.

**SEASON & HOURS:** Open for day use by reservation only.

**FACILITIES:** Restrooms and trails.

**CONTACT:** Irvine Ranch Land Reserve: 714-832-7478; www.irvineranchlandreserve.org.

The Irvine Ranch Land Reserve consists of 45,000 acres of natural land dedicated by the Irvine Company as open space. As many as a dozen other landowners and managers—including Orange County Harbors, Beaches, and Parks, the Nature Reserve of Orange County, and the Nature Conservancy—cooperatively manage pieces of the reserve. Most of the land accessible from the Santa Ana River is managed by the Nature Conservancy (TNC), which has done a tremendous job of balancing public access with ecological protection. To accomplish this, TNC has had to keep many areas of the reserve off limits to the public while non-intrusive routes were laid out. In addition, they have limited some types of use in some areas. For example, dogs are not allowed in most areas, and mountain biking is restricted to certain trails and roads.

From Gypsum Canyon, which at the time of this writing was being converted from mining to residential use, visitors can access the reserve on guided tours that climb and descend into and out of the beautiful canyons of the Santa Ana Mountains. The northern edge of the mountains and foothills are home to many sensitive and protected species, including mountain lions, American badgers, California gnatcatchers, and more.

Rare stands of native grassland, riparian corridors, old-growth oak woodlands, and high-quality coastal sage scrub can all be found on a

**One of the wildest places in Orange County, Irvine Ranch Land Reserve**

single dayhike in the reserve. For those feeling very adventurous, trails leading from the river into the reserve can be used to connect to the ocean at Laguna Beach or even farther south via the Cleveland National Forest to San Diego County.

# Anaheim Wetlands

**HIGHLIGHTS:** Anaheim Wetlands is home to the only interpretive information in Santa Ana Canyon.

**ACCESS:** The Anaheim Wetlands can be found
between the river and La Palma Ave., east of
Weir Canyon Road.

**SEASON & HOURS:** Sunrise to sunset.

**FACILITIES:** Interpretive displays and trails.

**CONTACT:** Oak Canyon Nature Center: 714-998-8380;
www.anaheim.net/ocnc.

At Anaheim Wetlands, a 2-acre site that comprises the west end of the wild riparian forest that covers the floor of Santa Ana Canyon, a small restoration project is in progress to mitigate the loss of similar habitat downstream. If it weren't for a few small signs and an interpretive display, the area would not stand out from the rest of the Santa Ana Canyon wilderness.

Mulefat, willow, and bulrush make up the bulk of vegetation in the area, but those who look hard may find an abundance of other native vegetation, including buckwheat, cottonwoods, coyote brush, bush lupine, and many annual wildflowers. As with any low-maintenance area, many exotic pest species such as castor bean and giant reed also have invaded the site.

An interpretive display describes the habitat and some of the wildlife species visitors may encounter in the area. The display is featured at a small turnout along the Santa Ana River Bikeway as it rises to meet La Palma Ave. The display was designed and is maintained by the Oak Canyon Nature Center.

# Yorba Regional Park

**HIGHLIGHTS:** At Yorba Regional Park, you can watch cormorants and terns fish in the lake, and an occasional kingfisher might just show up just after the lake has been stocked.

**ACCESS:** 7600 East La Palma Ave., Anaheim.

**SEASON & HOURS:** April through October, 7 AM to 8 PM; November through March, 7 AM to 6 PM.

**FACILITIES:** Restrooms, picnic areas, playgrounds, trails, sports fields, stocked fishing lakes, bike rentals, and horseshoe pits.

**CONTACT:** Yorba Regional Park: 714-973-6615 or 714-973-6838; www.ocparks.com/yorbapark.

This park is named after Bernardo Yorba, who owned the land for much of the 19th century as part of his 13,000-acre Rancho Cannon de Santa Ana, which was granted to him by the Mexican government.

Today, Yorba Regional Park comprises approximately 175 acres of manicured turf, mature trees, and lakes. The park was designed primarily to serve as a location for picnicking, however, many other activities are possible, including bicycling, fishing, volleyball, a par course, and baseball. Its function as a picnic grounds is still well served with dozens of shelters and hundreds of picnic tables shaded by mature pines, peppers, sycamores, and cottonwoods. A small city park borders Yorba Regional Park on the west end and includes softball fields. An unpaved parking lot designed as an equestrian staging area is farther west, but it often fills up during softball season because it is free to enter.

The series of four lakes totaling approximately 20 acres lie at the heart of the park and are connected by an artificial stream. The lakes are stocked by California Department of Fish and Game, and fishing is encouraged but requires a state license. Dozens of wood-duck boxes hang from trees surrounding the lake and appear to be successful; in late spring, wood ducks are numerous near the shore of the lake and in the river just outside the park. Small stands of cattail dot the lakeshore, giving it a natural appearance and providing habitat for migratory birds and fish.

The Santa Ana River can be accessed via numerous spur trails along the southern edge of the park. This reach of the Santa Ana River is bound by riprap grouted with concrete, but it maintains a soft bottom.

**The Santa Ana River Bikeway tops the northern levy at Yorba Regional Park.**

Regular flow through this area is moderate and encourages a braided, multichannel river with numerous sandbars and islands. Spring and summer provide opportunities to see cormorants, terns, and swallows. Black-necked stilts, avocets, and killdeer can be seen foraging in shallow water and on mudflats. Great blue herons, black-crowned night herons, and great egrets also are common here. Both paved and natural surface trails run between the river and Yorba Regional Park.

# Riverdale Park

**HIGHLIGHTS:** This urban park features easy river access, abundant urban wildlife, clean restrooms, and a casual atmosphere.

**ACCESS:** 4500 Riverdale Ave., Anaheim.

**SEASON & HOURS:** Sunrise to 10 PM.

**FACILITIES:** Restrooms, picnic areas, and sports fields.

**CONTACT:** Anaheim Parks: 714-765-5191; www.anaheim.net.

This approximately 8-acre neighborhood park includes both active and passive recreational facilities—for playing baseball, soccer, or just having a picnic. Because of its location and free parking, it is one of the best places to access the river along this reach, with excellent access to the Santa Ana River Trail. Mostly manicured turf surrounded by tall eucalyptus trees, this park is also great for picnics and quick outings to explore the river through Santa Ana Canyon.

The river at this location is soft bottom with riprap sides, and it is located on the upstream side of the Orange County Water District's recharge ponds, making this a nice entrance to the river for wildlife-watching. Egrets, herons, kingfishers, and osprey can all be observed along this reach of the river. Bring your binoculars, or, better yet, your spotting scope, because in evenings and early mornings, visitors are likely to see coyotes, bobcats, and raccoons hunting around the recharge ponds on the north side of the river.

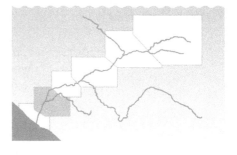

# ORANGE COUNTY COASTAL PLAIN

The Orange County Coastal Plain is, at first glance, the least wild and most urban of all the river reaches. This is not to say, however, that the casual explorer will not find wildlife, native vegetation, or plenty of exciting discoveries.

The Orange County Water District uses the upper portion of this reach for groundwater recharge operations. In some areas, it appears as though the river has two distinct channels. Numerous settling ponds dot the north side of the river in the area between the 91 Freeway and Ball Road. An elaborate system of inflatable dams, gates, and dykes moves water to the best locations for percolation into the Santa Ana River aquifer, the most heavily used and managed groundwater basin on the planet. Approximately 65 percent of the water used by Orange County residents and visitors comes out of the ground under the Santa Ana River.

This is also the reach of river where flood-control efforts are the hardest in design and material. At the very least, this reach of river has riprap-armored levies. At most, the river is confined to a trapezoidal concrete channel. The one major exception is at the Riverview Golf Course, which is viewed as a model by those looking to "green" the lower river. Though the golf course appears to be unprotected, it was engineered to meet the same specifications as the river below it. Twenty or more feet of soil were removed, and then riprap and concrete were placed along the levies. The soil was then returned and the site was landscaped to appear as though it was a completely natural waterway.

For this roughly 1-mile reach, short, cropped green grass stretches from levy to levy, creating a gently sloped channel with a meandering stream course through the middle. Trees dot the area, in some places forming a riparian forest crossing the channel.

Above Riverview Golf Course, the river has a sand bottom with reinforced riprap walls. Trails line both sides of the river; one is multi-use, and the other is a bikeway. The bike trail and related landscaping create a sort of linear park complete with rest stops, drinking fountains, restrooms, and picnic tables. Numerous pocket-sized neighborhood parks line the river, providing parking and additional access to the river.

Below Riverview Golf Course, the river channel becomes hardened with concrete walls and bottom. The Army Corps of Engineers has, however, as part of the Santa Ana River Mainstem Project, created a more natural greenway along the bikeway. Here, native trees and shrubs line the trail and large boulders dot the area and can be used for seating as well as visual enhancement. For those willing to move slowly along this stretch, many native birds and reptiles can be found taking advantage of the landscape improvements, which have created a tiny biological corridor along the river. Similar treatments are planned for the multiuse trail on the opposite side of the river, but at the time of this writing, a pipeline installation project was underway there.

Many parks and open-space areas are located along the river in this area, and the numerous cities that line the river's banks here are planning for many additional visual and environmental improvements.

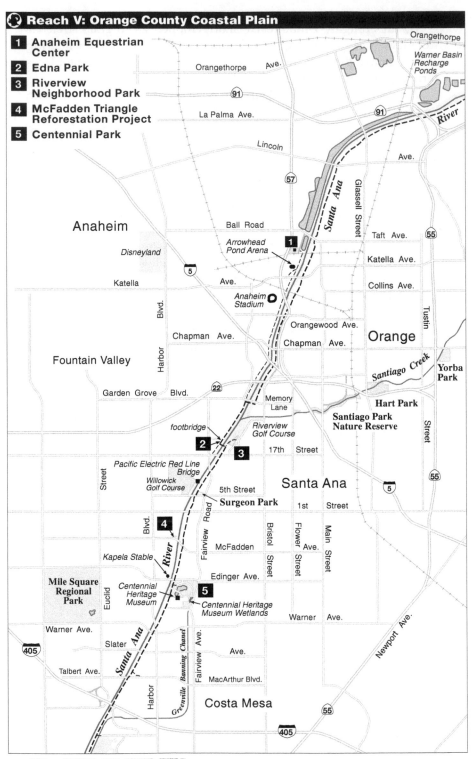

# Reach V: Orange County Coastal Plain

**1** Anaheim Equestrian Center

**2** Edna Park

**3** Riverview Neighborhood Park

**4** McFadden Triangle Reforestation Project

**5** Centennial Park

Orangethorpe

Warner Basin Recharge Ponds

Orangethorpe Ave.

(91)

La Palma Ave.

(91)

River

Lincoln

Ave.

Anaheim

(57)

Santa Ana

Glassell Street

Ball Road

Taft Ave. (55)

Arrowhead Pond Arena **1**

Disneyland

Katella Ave.

(5)

Collins Ave.

Katella Ave.

Anaheim Stadium

Blvd.

Harbor

Tustin

Orangewood Ave.

Chapman Ave.

Chapman Ave.

Orange

Fountain Valley

Santiago Creek

Yorba Park

Garden Grove Blvd. (22)

Memory Lane

Hart Park

footbridge

Riverview Golf Course

Santiago Park Nature Reserve

**2**

**3**

17th Street

Street

Pacific Electric Red Line Bridge

(55)

Willowick Golf Course

Street

5th Street

Santa Ana

(5)

Surgeon Park

1st Street

Blvd. **4**

Fairview Road

McFadden Ave.

Bristol Street

Flower Street

Main Street

River

Kapela Stable

Edinger Ave.

Mile Square Regional Park

Euclid

Centennial Heritage Museum

Centennial Heritage Museum Wetlands

**5**

Warner Ave.

Warner Ave.

Newport Ave.

(405)

Slater

Santa Ana

Greenville Banning Channel

Fairview Ave.

Ave.

Talbert Ave.

Harbor

MacArthur Blvd.

Costa Mesa

(55)

(405)

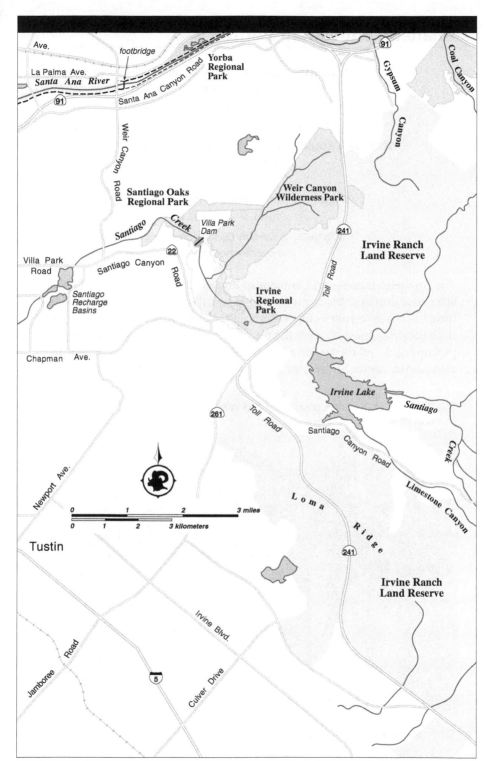

# Anaheim Equestrian Center

**HIGHLIGHTS:** Escape from the bustling urban center just outside the fence to watch children discover the relaxed equestrian lifestyle.

**ACCESS:** 13705 South Sanderson Street, Anaheim.

**SEASON & HOURS:** Monday through Friday, 10 AM to 6 PM; Saturday, 9 AM to 5 PM; Sunday, 10 AM to 4 PM.

**FACILITIES:** Restrooms, equestrian boarding facilities, classes, and a feed and tack store.

**CONTACT:** Anaheim Equestrian Center: 714-535-3510; www.ranchodelriostables.com.

The Anaheim Equestrian Center, also known as Rancho del Rio Stables, is a community center as much as it is boarding facility for horses. Visiting the 5-acre center is like stepping back to a time when horses and the equestrian lifestyle were the norm along the Santa Ana River. Dusty pickup trucks fill the parking lot and several large cats sleep on the rustic wooden porch of the center's office and store. Two large arenas, a

**The Rancho del Rio store creates an Old West atmosphere at the Anaheim Equestrian Center.**

campfire circle, and various early 20th century artifacts rest between rows of pipe corrals and box stables.

In 2000, the Orange County Water District was threatening to convert this area to a groundwater-recharge basin, but the city of Anaheim and the water district came to recognize the historic and educational value of the facility and spared the grounds for the foreseeable future.

In addition to boarding and training horses, del Rio also provides classes for the local recreation departments, including Anaheim, Orange, and Santa Ana. Children as young as 4 learn to groom, clean up after, and ride horses—increasingly rare opportunities for the more than 1 million people who live within a 10-mile radius of the center.

This site is one of only a few places on the lower Santa Ana where equestrians can access the river directly from where they keep their horses. If you'd like to bring your own horse for a ride along the river, call the stables first to make arrangements.

# Edna Park

**HIGHLIGHTS:** Edna Park provides easy river access in the middle of this Orange County reach, making it a great starting point for trips upstream and down.

**ACCESS:** 2140 West Edna Street, Santa Ana.

**SEASON & HOURS:** 7 AM to 9 PM.

**FACILITIES:** Restrooms, playground, and picnic area.

**CONTACT:** Santa Ana Parks, Recreation, and Community Services Agency: 714-571-4200; www.ci.santa-ana.ca.us/parks.

The linear 2-acre Edna Park, just below the western levy, follows the Santa Ana River for approximately a quarter mile. A row of native riparian trees and bunch grasses adorn the levy slope. California sycamore, alder, and Fremont cottonwood make up the thin, forested strip. Additional habitat restoration is planned for the southern end of the park.

Emerald green turf carpets most of the park and picnic sites are provided under the shade of mature sycamores. These are within site of the playgrounds and restrooms, making Edna Park an excellent riverbank location for family outings.

When Edna Park was first developed in the late 1970s, it included equestrian amenities (water trough and hitching post), but those have since been removed. The city of Santa Ana, in an agreement with Orange County, will encourage equestrian use of Edna Park and may eventually replace the original amenities.

Another attribute of Edna Park is its location next to southern limits of Riverview Golf Course and the regional hiking and biking trail. Water often ponds up here before making its way onto the concrete channel that runs down the middle of the river for the 7 miles below the golf course. Pacific tree frogs, mallards, and shore birds are common along this stretch of the river. If visitors are patient, a peek at resident coyotes and red fox is also possible.

# Riverview Neighborhood Park

**HIGHLIGHTS:** Easy access to the Santa Ana River Trail and a great view across the Riverview Golf Course make Riverview Park seem much larger than it really is.

**ACCESS:** 1817 West 21 Street, Santa Ana.

**SEASON & HOURS:** 7 AM to 9 PM.

**FACILITIES:** Restrooms, playgrounds, picnic area, and sports fields.

**CONTACT:** Santa Ana Parks, Recreation, and Community Services Agency: 714-571-4200; www.santa-ana.ca.us/parks.

Considered a neighborhood park by the city of Santa Ana, Riverview is also an excellent place to access one of the nicest reaches of river in Santa Ana. Located across the river from Edna Park on the east levy at the south end of Riverview Golf Course, this 10-acre park provides excellent picnic sites and other amenities typical of a neighborhood park.

Riverview Park feels much larger than it is. Bordering Riverview Golf Course with only a chain-link fence separating them, the view from the park extends for more than a half mile across the golf course and Santa Ana River.

Riverview Neighborhood Park is anything but a natural park. Lightly forested with a mix of eucalyptus, elm, pepper, and carob trees that shade the closely cropped turf, this is not the park for those seeking a look at the historic riparian forests that once lined the river. It does, however, provide visitors with access to the river, as well as connections to the Crest to Coast Trails. It also has great views of the willow woodlands and ponds found within the golf course. Shore birds such as black-necked stilts, American avocets, and killdeer are common along this stretch, which is also home to red fox and coyotes.

Although it fills up during Little League season and occasionally on weekends, the park is mostly quiet during the week.

# McFadden Triangle Reforestation Project

**HIGHLIGHTS:** At McFadden, an urban community is building a forest, one tree sapling at a time. You can come here to watch it grow.

**ACCESS:** McFadden Ave. where Susan Street dead-ends. The site is on the north side of McFadden Ave. and the west side of the Santa Ana River.

**SEASON & HOURS:** 7 AM to sunset.

**FACILITIES:** There are currently no facilities here, but future plans include shaded seating and interpretive displays.

**CONTACT:** Santa Ana Parks, Recreation, and Community Services Agency: 714-571-4200; www.ci.santa-ana.ca.us/parks.

Once a vacant lot dotted with piles of illegally dumped debris and trash, this half-acre site has been transformed into a riparian forest. More than 80 trees now grow on the property, which can be accessed from McFadden Ave., Susan Street, or the Santa Ana River.

Cottonwood, willow, alder, sycamore, and oak of various sizes comprise this forest. A few native grasses and shrubs also grow on the site. The trees will eventually reach 80 feet or more and will provide excellent shade for the many pedestrians, cyclists, and equestrians who pass this location.

The site was planted by volunteers, and it is maintained through a partnership between the city of Santa Ana and the Santa Anita Neighborhood Association. The project was supported financially by the neighborhood Wal-Mart, and the trees were provided free of charge by the Shadetree Partnership Nursery.

**A future forest grows at Santa Ana's McFadden Triangle.**

# Centennial Park

**HIGHLIGHTS:** This park is one of the best birding sites in Santa Ana. The lake attracts numerous water species, including American white pelicans, osprey, cormorants, and more. The mature trees are great for migrating warblers and raptors. In the early evening, visitors can watch bats feed over the lake.

**ACCESS:** 3000 West Edinger Ave., Santa Ana. The park is on Edinger between the Santa Ana River and Fairview Street.

**SEASON & HOURS:** 7 AM to 9 PM.

**FACILITIES:** Restrooms, picnic area, trails, sports fields, stocked fishing lake, and skate park.

**CONTACT:** Santa Ana Parks, Recreation, and Community Services Agency: 714-571-4200; www.ci.santa-ana.ca.us/parks.

This 75-acre park was once a regional park shared by the city and county, but through a joint-use agreement between the city and the Santa Ana Unified School District, a science high school was constructed on 10 acres of the park, reducing its acreage below the county standard for regional parks.

**The 10-acre lake at Centennial Park**

The park still contains a 10-acre lake stocked with rainbow trout in winter, extensive picnic areas, softball diamonds, a large soccer complex, and a skate park. A meandering trail follows a short riparian corridor that connects to some of the last remaining freshwater marsh habitat in the city. The marsh habitat is outside of the park, but it can be accessed through the Centennial Heritage Museum (see page 217 for access details).

Mature trees grace most of the park, providing adequate shade for picnicking and bird-watching. Additional habitat restoration activities are taking place in the park with the future goal of reconnecting the marsh habitat at the museum to the river via the riparian corridor. Santa Ana College also maintains a satellite campus at the park, and the Santa Ana Fire Department manages a training facility here in conjunction with the college's firefighting academy.

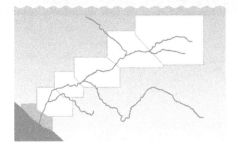

# ORANGE COAST AND THE RIVER MOUTH

The Santa Ana River has influenced the Orange County landscape more than almost anything else. For hundreds of thousands of years, the river has eroded high mountains and deposited the sediment in what is now Orange County. At times, the river would scour the landscape, stripping the forest and shrublands. Other times, the river would flood the area, creating huge freshwater marshes as well as some of the best farming conditions on the planet. Aerial and satellite photos show at least two different historic channels that the river followed to the ocean, and for this reason, both historic Santa Ana River estuaries are described in this section.

Today, this section of river is a mix of the natural and the engineered. The channel walls are vertical, concrete, and at least 30 feet high. The river bottom is sandy, silty, and muddy and is influenced by tidal changes. Sand-collecting operations compete with shorebirds and an occasional bald eagle for resources. Historic wetlands have been reduced, but restoration efforts show signs of success.

Numerous parks and open space areas are located along the levies here, and they range in style, use, and access. A major effort is underway to connect all of these areas to create a coastal park of more than 1000 acres that would support almost every imaginable use. Dubbed the Orange Coast River Park, this effort partners two cities, the county of Orange, and numerous private entities.

The bikeway and the multiuse trail are complete in this area and are located on opposite sides of the river. They terminate at the beach where surf, sand, and sun come together to greet the river and its travelers.

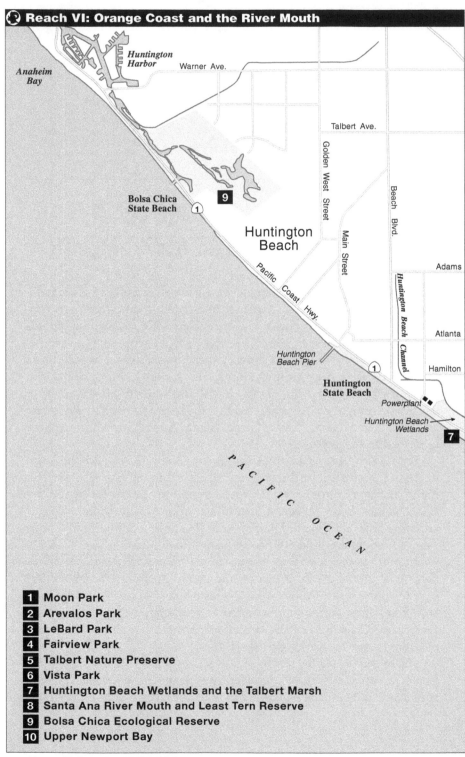

*Anaheim Bay*

*Huntington Harbor*

Warner Ave.

Talbert Ave.

Golden West Street

Beach Blvd.

**Bolsa Chica State Beach**

**9**

①

Huntington Beach

Main Street

Adams

Pacific Coast Hwy.

*Huntington Beach Channel*

Atlanta

Huntington Beach Pier

①

Hamilton

**Huntington State Beach**

Powerplant ◆■

Huntington Beach Wetlands

**7**

P A C I F I C   O C E A N

1 Moon Park
2 Arevalos Park
3 LeBard Park
4 Fairview Park
5 Talbert Nature Preserve
6 Vista Park
7 Huntington Beach Wetlands and the Talbert Marsh
8 Santa Ana River Mouth and Least Tern Reserve
9 Bolsa Chica Ecological Reserve
10 Upper Newport Bay

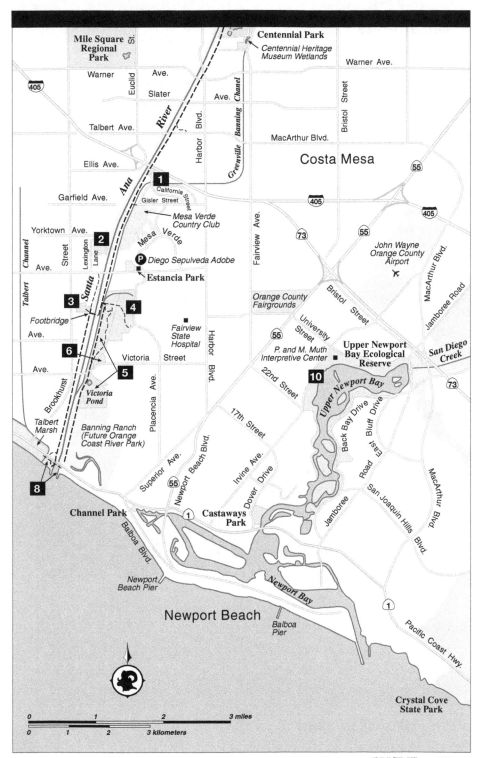

Mile Square
Regional
Park

Centennial Park

Centennial Heritage
Museum Wetlands

Warner Ave.

Warner Ave.

Euclid St.

Ave.

Slater Ave.

Bristol Street

Talbert Ave.

Harbor Blvd.

Greenville Banning Chanel

MacArthur Blvd.

Costa Mesa

405

55

Ellis Ave.

**1**

California Street

Garfield Ave.

Gisler Street

405

55

Mesa Verde
Country Club

Fairview Ave.

405

Yorktown Ave.

**2**

Mesa Verde

73

55

John Wayne
Orange County
Airport

Lexington Lane

P Diego Sepulveda Adobe

Ave.

Street

Santa

**Estancia Park**

MacArthur Blvd.

Talbert Channel

**3**

**4**

Fairview
State
Hospital

Orange County
Fairgrounds

Bristol Street

Jamboree Road

Footbridge

Ave.

University Street

San Diego Creek

**6**

Victoria

P. and M. Muth
Interpretive Center

**Upper Newport
Bay Ecological
Reserve**

Ave.

**5**

Street

73

Brookhurst

Victoria
Pond

Placentia Ave.

Harbor Blvd.

22nd Street

**10**

Upper Newport Bay

Back Bay Drive

Talbert
Marsh

Banning Ranch
(Future Orange
Coast River Park)

17th Street

East Bluff Drive

**8**

Superior Ave.

Newport Beach Blvd.

Irvine Ave.

Dover Drive

Road

San Joaquin Hills Blvd.

**Channel Park**

55

1

**Castaways
Park**

Jamboree

MacArthur Blvd.

Balboa Blvd.

Newport
Beach Pier

Newport Bay

1

**Newport Beach**

Balboa
Pier

Pacific Coast Hwy.

**Crystal Cove
State Park**

| 0 | 1 | 2 | 3 miles |
| 0 | 1 | 2 | 3 kilometers |

# Moon Park

**HIGHLIGHTS:** Whimsical Moon Park also has a seamless connection to the river trail.

**ACCESS:** 3377 California Street, Costa Mesa.

**SEASON & HOURS:** Sunrise to 9 PM.

**FACILITIES:** Picnic area and playground.

**CONTACT:** Costa Mesa Parks Department: 714-754-5300; www.ci.costa-mesa.ca.us.

Moon is a 2-acre neighborhood park found directly along the Santa Ana River Trail. The park takes its name from the crater-covered, moonlike concrete dome structure rising from the north end of the park. This popular and unique climbing structure is only one of several playground facilities in the park.

Traditional play equipment is located on either side of the "moon," and picnic tables are located nearby. All of the half a dozen or so picnic tables in the park are shaded by large ficus trees that border the rolling turf covering most of the park.

Moon Park borders the river, and only the trail and a native-landscape-covered levy separate the two. Unlike most neighborhood and small parks along the river, Moon Park has no fence or other structure to keep trail users from entering the park anywhere they want. This is popular with many cyclists and walkers who like to take breaks in the shade of the park.

**The "moon" at Moon Park**

# Arevalos Park

**HIGHLIGHTS:** From Arevalos, you have the unique opportunity to watch from above as shore birds scurry along the river bottom.

**ACCESS:** 10440 Shalon Street, Huntington Beach.

**SEASON & HOURS:** Sunrise to sunset.

**FACILITIES:** Playground.

**CONTACT:** City of Huntington Beach Parks Department: 714-536-5486; www.ci.huntington-beach.ca.us.

Arevalos Park, a 2-acre sliver of land sandwiched between Pegasus School and the western levy of the river in Huntington Beach, is a welcome public space under Southern California Edison power lines and between nurseries, which occupy most of this right-of-way.

It is obviously a neighborhood park, as it has no restrooms or picnic tables and it shares parking with the school when it's not in session. It does, however, have a playground, an acre of turf, and, most importantly, access to the unpaved maintenance road and multiuse trail. From this trail, visitors can move upstream and down for as many as 5 miles. And because the walls of the river channel are vertical here, users of the trail look right down onto the soft bottom and sand flats of the river. Killdeer and other shore birds are common in this area and are easily viewed from the levy.

**Arevalos is a neighborhood park with great river access.**

# LeBard Park

**HIGHLIGHTS:** LeBard Park provides easy access to the river trail, and in summer there are plenty of cheap seats for ball games.

**ACCESS:** 20461 Cramer Street, Huntington Beach.

**SEASON & HOURS:** Sunrise to sunset.

**FACILITIES:** Restrooms, playground, picnic area, sports fields, lighted tennis courts, and club house.

**CONTACT:** Huntington Beach Parks Department: 714-536-5486; www.ci.huntington-beach.ca.us.

This neighborhood park is home to Seaview Little League, and they take their game seriously, as the banner above the main field attests: DESTINATION WILLIAMSPORT, HOME OF THE LITTLE LEAGUE WORLD SERIES. The baseball diamonds are of various sizes and are easily the nicest Little League facilities this author has seen.

The part of the park that is not used for baseball is mostly consumed by tennis courts, a playground, and clubhouse; however, its eastern end abuts the river and contains remnant habitat including wetlands. Picnic tables are scattered about the roughly 5-acre park.

When it's not baseball season, there is ample parking, and the site provides excellent access to the river trail. This is a great place to park when trying to beat the crowds at Huntington State Beach. The ocean is less than a 1-mile pedal down the river trail, and it crosses no traffic.

LeBard Park connects with nearly 20 acres of Southern California Edison property along the river. The Huntington Beach Conservancy and Orange Coast River Park have been working to acquire, through lease, some of these areas. Much of the land is currently being used by nurseries as growing grounds, but many have no title or permits securing their use.

**The LeBard Bridge**

# Fairview Park

**HIGHLIGHTS:** Views from the bluff of the coast, river, and vernal pools in full bloom make Fairview Park worth the visit in any season.

**ACCESS:** 2525 Placentia Ave. (between Adams Ave. and Victoria Street), Costa Mesa.

**SEASON & HOURS:** Sunrise to 10 PM.

**FACILITIES:** Restrooms, interpretive displays, picnic area, trails, model trains, and model airplanes.

**CONTACT:** Costa Mesa Parks Department: 714-754-5300; www.ci.costa-mesa.ca.us.
Fairview Park Friends: 714-754-5698.

Divided by Placentia Ave., the 210-acre Fairview Park is largely undeveloped. West of Placentia Ave. are 155 acres of natural rolling parkland crisscrossed with single-track trails. Another 55 acres are located east of the road. The park should be complete in 2010, at which time it will include native habitat, an interpretive center, and 2 miles of hiking trails with connections to the Talbert Nature Preserve, Santa Ana River Trail, and the Pacific Ocean.

This bluff-top nature park is already full of hidden treasures. As you enter the parking lot to the west of Placentia Ave., you'll encounter a small strip of bright green turf, a stone picnic shelter and asphalt trail. Beyond the 60-foot manicured beltway, however, a dense growth of mulefat, sagebrush, and mustard cover the ripples of former sea-bottom sediment cut away over centuries by the Santa Ana River.

Once home to one of the largest Native American villages in Orange County, the park now hosts model glider and train enthusiasts in addition to the nature lovers. Rare vernal pools top the southern end of the bluff and are home to the protected San Diego fairy shrimp. A narrow-gauge railroad circumnavigates the eastern portion of the park.

**The bluffs at Fairview Park**

# Talbert Nature Preserve

**HIGHLIGHTS:** During a visit to Talbert Nature Preserve, you may see coyotes in the middle of the day, or you can enjoy birding around Victoria Pond.

**ACCESS:** 10151 Victoria Street, Costa Mesa. The best way to get into the nature preserve is to park at Fairview Park; see page 139 for directions. The preserve can be accessed from Victoria Street, but parking is limited here.

**SEASON AND HOURS:** Sunrise to sunset.

**FACILITIES:** Restrooms, interpretive displays, picnic area, and equestrian facilities.

**CONTACT:** Talbert Nature Preserve: 949-923-2250; www.ocparks.com/talbert.

Descending the bluffs from Fairview Park on the steep paved trail or by one of the steeper, rugged, and deteriorating shoots, visitors discover the Talbert Nature Preserve. Divided into two distinct sections, Talbert North is made up of 91.5 acres and Talbert South is another 88.5 acres. The two are bisected by Victoria Ave.

**Entrance to Talbert Nature Preserve North**

**Looking over the grasslands of Talbert Nature Preserve**

Access to this reserve is only by trail via Fairview Park, 19th Street, or from the Santa Ana River Trail. Adequate public parking can be found at Fairview Park, but you can also try your luck at Vista Park (see page 142).

The 180-acre Talbert Nature Preserve consists of restored habitat, including coastal sand dune, riparian woodland, grassland, and coastal sage scrub. Victoria Pond, located in the southern reserve, is an open 1-acre pond that has been known to serve large flocks of white pelicans. Wetlands can be found on both sides of the reserve. Large, open meadows occupy the northern reserve.

Several miles of decomposed granite trails wind through the habitats and are popular with runners, cyclists, and nature watchers. A picnic area with restrooms, manicured grass, and tables is also available at the northern reserve.

# Vista Park

**HIGHLIGHTS:** Just as the name of the park implies, Vista is a great place to get a nice view of the river or just to take a break.

**ACCESS:** 1200 Victoria Street, Costa Mesa.

**SEASON & HOURS:** Sunrise to 10 PM.

**FACILITIES:** Restrooms, playgrounds, and picnic area.

**CONTACT:** Costa Mesa Parks Department: 714-754-5300; www.ci.costa-mesa.ca.us.

This small bluff-top park is named for the spectacular view of the river, the coast, and the city of Huntington Beach. Perched 100 feet above the Talbert Nature Preserve North, near the intersection of Victoria Ave. and Hamilton Street, the 2-acre park is an ideal location for viewing the lower river. It's easy to imagine why this area was so popular with the indigenous people who called this area home for eons prior to construction of the condominiums that now surround the park site.

The park is a popular place for picnicking, with a half dozen picnic sites scattered about and shaded by large native and exotic trees. A paved trail meanders around the perimeter of the park and connects to most of the picnic sites. The trail bounds a large turf area great for pick-up games of Frisbee, catch, and maybe even soccer. Its greatest attributes, however, are its looping trails and park benches overlooking the bluff and offering views that stretch for 40 miles on a clear day.

**The view from Vista Park**

# Huntington Beach Wetlands
# and the Talbert Marsh

**HIGHLIGHTS:** Watching the changes in activity at the marshes as the tide rises and falls is a great way to pass the time at the Huntington Beach Wetlands.

**ACCESS:** The Huntington Beach Wetlands and Talbert Marsh are located opposite Pacific Coast Hwy. between the Santa Ana River and Newland Street. The wetlands can be accessed from the Santa Ana River or by parking at Huntington State Beach.

**SEASON & HOURS:** Sunrise to sunset.

**FACILITIES:** Trails and interpretive signage.

**CONTACT:** Huntington Beach Wetlands Conservancy: 714-963-2123; www.hbwc.org.

Much of the Huntington Beach Wetlands appear to be abandoned—there are no signs or other distinguishing human features that would attract passers-by on the Pacific Coast Hwy. But those who do stop to explore the tidal channels, mudflats, and ponds of this nearly 200-acre complex will quickly see that the wetlands are not abandoned. Rather, they are dynamic and alive in every sense.

Talbert Marsh, immediately north of the river, is fed by the Talbert Channel and flushed by tidal changes. The Army Corps of Engineers restored this 40-acre wetland in the 1990s and it now serves as a refuge for 100 species of birds, fish, and other wildlife.

As visitors continue north, either on Pacific Coast Hwy. or on trail, another 150 acres of saltwater, brackish, and freshwater marshes expand and contract inland from the coast. Paved and unpaved trails lead the explorer around each of these. Terns dive for food while curlews slice at the silt and sandpipers dart along the shoreline. Small islands and mudflats provide shelter for nesting birds, while the occasional osprey or bald eagle can be seen fishing the area.

In addition to providing important habitat and flood protection, the Huntington Beach Wetlands also give human visitors a visual relief from the dense coastal development that has choked so much of the Orange County coast.

# Santa Ana River Mouth
# and Least Tern Reserve

**HIGHLIGHTS:** Come here in the spring to watch the least terns during nesting season, or come to lie on the beach and watch the sunset at the river mouth.

**ACCESS:** Located where the Santa Ana River meets the Pacific Ocean at Pacific Coast Hwy. Huntington State Beach is on the north shore, and Newport Beach is on the south shore. On-street metered parking is available on the Newport side, and parking is available at Huntington State Beach for $4. Larger vehicles may be required to pay additional fees up to $14.

**SEASON & HOURS:** Sunrise to 10 PM.

**FACILITIES:** Restrooms and the end of the Santa Ana River Trail.

**CONTACT:** County of Orange: 714-834-5173; Huntington State Beach: 714-536-1454; www.parks.ca.gove/?page_id=643.

Tucked between two stone jetties where it must navigate over and around a series of sandbars, the brackish water of the Santa Ana River slides into the Pacific Ocean with little more than a ripple where the two waters unite. A popular surf spot known locally as the river jetties, this physical boundary between Newport Beach and Huntington Beach is also a popular sunbathing beach that typifies the SoCal experience.

Houses line the beach to the south of the river on the Newport Beach side and are home to the rich and famous or those willing to go deep into debt to appear rich and famous. Many of the houses also rent by the week during the summer, serving college students and families seeking a beachfront vacation.

Immediately north of the river, a very different scene greets visitors. A slightly rusted chain-link fence topped by barbed wire excludes sun worshippers from spreading out their blankets. Rather, it protects a different kind of beachgoer—the endangered least tern. This reserve protects one of the bird's largest breeding populations in Southern California.

**A quiet sunrise at the Santa Ana River mouth**

The fence serves a second vital service to river-mouth visitors. On any given summer day, as many as 100 bicycles may be locked to it. The Pacific Coast Trail, a regional recreational hiking and biking trail, runs between Pacific Coast Hwy. and the reserve in Huntington Beach, and right in front of the beachside homes on the Newport side. Locals call the trail here the "Boardwalk."

The mudflats that form along the river at its mouth attract curlews, western sandpipers, and other shorebirds. Terns and pelicans dive in its waters and a half dozen gull species scavenge from all the other visitors to the Santa Ana River mouth, particularly the humans. Fishermen often cast into the surf here.

# Bolsa Chica Ecological Reserve

**HIGHLIGHTS:** The mild coastal conditions and a chance to see several endangered species make Bolsa Chica a great destination for short hikes and longer explorations.

**ACCESS:** 18000 Pacific Coast Hwy. or 3842 Warner Ave. in Huntington Beach.

**SEASON & HOURS:** 6 AM to 8 PM.

**FACILITIES:** Restrooms, trails, and an interpretive center.

**CONTACT:** Amigos de Bolsa Chica: 714-840-1575; www.amigosdebolsachica.org. Bolsa Chica Conservancy: 714-846-1114; www.bolsachica.org. Bolsa Chica Land Trust: 714-846-1001; wwwbolsachicalandtrust.org.

Bolsa Chica Ecological Reserve is composed of 1187 acres of wetlands, including saltwater marsh and coastal dunes, and 118 acres of upland habitat on the lower mesa. The extensive reserve has limited access and only a couple miles of trail, however, it only takes a few steps from either parking lot to become absorbed in the environment and to begin seeing why this reserve is so important.

Visitors can count on seeing at least one threatened or endangered species on every trip. On a recent visit, I identified more than a dozen species of birds and stopped counting Belding's savannah sparrows because they were so numerous. California least terns, another endangered species, black-necked stilts, and numerous grebes were identified before the first bend in the boardwalk. On clear days, the view of Saddleback Mountain is one of the best in Orange County, making it easy to imagine what it must have been like a century earlier when the Santa Ana River was connected to the wetlands at Bolsa Chica.

Bolsa Chica has great historical significance as well as ecological importance. Home to the Tongva/Gabrielino nation for at least the past 8000 years, the mesa at Bolsa Chica is an important archeological location where, as early as the 1930s, studies uncovered many important artifacts and information. It was also home to the Bolsa Chica Gun Club, a hunting establishment started in the late 1800s. By the 1920s, oil had been discovered at Bolsa Chica and the area was further altered.

**A volunteer describes the restoration at the Bolsa Chica wetlands.**

By 2005, the tireless efforts of three nonprofit groups (Amigos de Bolsa Chica, Bolsa Chica Conservancy, and the Bolsa Chica Land Trust) had succeeded in securing more than $60 million in environmental mitigation from development of the Long Beach Harbor. The expansive restoration project will return formerly drained and dried oil fields back to saltwater marsh. In August 2006, the Pacific Ocean again flowed into the Bolsa Chica for the first time since the 1890s, rewatering the entire wetlands complex with tidal flows when the berm separating the wetlands from the ocean was removed.

# Upper Newport Bay

**HIGHLIGHTS:** Come here to see the birds and the many spectacular views from anywhere in the bay.

**ACCESS:** There are several ways to access Upper Newport Bay, including at the 1100 block of Back Bay Drive (a short loop road) west off of Jamboree Road, and via the Peter and Mary Muth Interpretive Center at 2301 University Drive in Newport Beach.

**SEASON & HOURS:** Back Bay Drive access is open sunrise to sunset. Peter and Mary Muth Interpretive Center is open Tuesday through Sunday, 10 AM to 4 PM.

**FACILITIES:** Restrooms, informational displays, and trails.

**CONTACT:** California Department of Fish and Game: 949-640-9956; www.dfg.ca.gov/lands/er/-region5/uppernewport.
Orange County Harbors, Beaches, and Parks: 949-923-2290; www.ocparks.gov.

Upper Newport Bay is a large tidal estuary originally sculpted centuries earlier by the Santa Ana River. Today, San Diego Creek flows into the bay, which is still one of the most spectacular views in Orange County. So spectacular is the scene from atop the sedimentary bluffs that many of the region's rich and famous have chosen to live here. It was this desire to develop the area that led to its preservation.

The protected area in Upper Newport Bay totals approximately 1000 acres. California Department of Fish and Game manages 750 acres as the Upper Newport Bay Ecological Reserve, while the county of Orange maintains the 150-acre Upper Newport Bay Nature Preserve. The city of Newport Beach, the Irvine Company, and local homeowner associations manage additional lands.

In addition to the views, Upper Newport Bay also is popular with wildlife—birds in particular. More than 200 species can be counted here and as many as 50,000 individuals may comb the shore and float the waters of the bay in winter. Among the avian numbers are endangered California clapper rails, California least terns, and brown pelicans. Belding's savannah sparrows, horned larks, and cooper's hawks are often seen in the brush of the uplands around the bay.

**The Upper Newport Bay Ecological Reserve as seen from on top of the Muth Center**

Miles of paved and unpaved trails circumnavigate the protected area, and many of the trails have interpretive displays along them. For those wishing to know more about the bay, take one of the trails to the Peter and Mary Muth Interpretive Center (949-923-2290; www.newportbay.org). Because the 8000-square-foot center is built into the bluff, people often don't even see it from the center's own parking lot. Displays inside teach about the bay's ecology and its many inhabitants. When visiting the center, ask one of the knowledgeable staff to show the video that depicts the bay throughout the year.

You can also see the Upper Newport Bay by non-motorized boat. The Newport Bay Naturalists, a nonprofit interpretive organization that helps provide programming at the bay, offers canoe tours, and individuals can ply the waters of the bay in designated areas. Check with Department of Fish and Game or Orange County park rangers for more information on access.

# TRIBUTARIES

The Santa Ana River has dozens of tributary streams, some small, and others, like Mill Creek or Santiago Creek, quite large. Sometimes these tributaries carry great amounts of water and appear to be rivers in their own right.

Regardless of their size, length, or volume, these tributaries always play important roles in the function of the Santa Ana River watershed. Just like the river, tributary streams provide flood conveyance, wildlife habitat, groundwater recharge, and recreational opportunities. Tributaries often provide services equal to, but on a smaller scale than, those of the river.

Many of the tributary streams, like those in the San Bernardino Mountains, are tiny and may not even be named. Downstream on the floodplain, some streams may have been diverted, channeled, or forced into culverts where they are limited to flood-control functions. These streams are given names like the Greenville Banning Channel or, worse yet, receive nothing more than a number on the counties' flood-control maps.

Other tributaries remain in various states of natural or wild. Some have riprap-reinforced slopes or concrete walls, and a few may even be trapezoidal channels for some distance along their paths to the river. None of the tributaries below the headwaters are without human influence, though a couple may have stretches that are still in a completely wild condition.

Some of the more familiar tributaries include Mill Creek, San Timoteo Creek, Plunge and Day creeks, and Cajon Wash, which flow from the San Bernardino Mountains. To the west, three forks of Lytle Creek—Cucamonga Creek, Etiwanda Creek, and San Antonio Creek—flow

*left:* **Mill Creek and the Valley of the Falls**

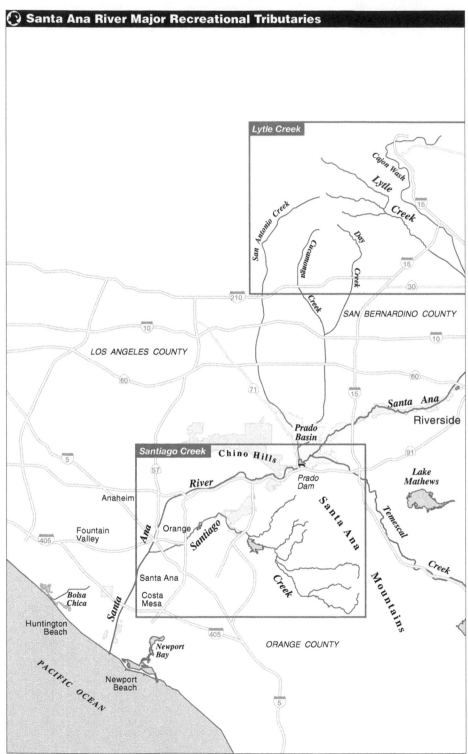

Lytle Creek

Cajon Wash

Lytle

San Antonio Creek

Creek

Cucamonga

Day

Creek

Creek

210

15

15

30

SAN BERNARDINO COUNTY

10

10

LOS ANGELES COUNTY

60

60

71

15

Santa Ana

Riverside

Prado
Basin

Santiago Creek

Chino Hills

5

57

River

Prado
Dam

Lake
Mathews

91

Anaheim

Ana

Orange

Santiago

Santa Ana

Temescal

Fountain
Valley

405

Creek

Santa Ana

Costa
Mesa

Creek

Mountains

Bolsa
Chica

Santa

Huntington
Beach

405

ORANGE COUNTY

PACIFIC

Newport
Bay

5

Newport
Beach

OCEAN

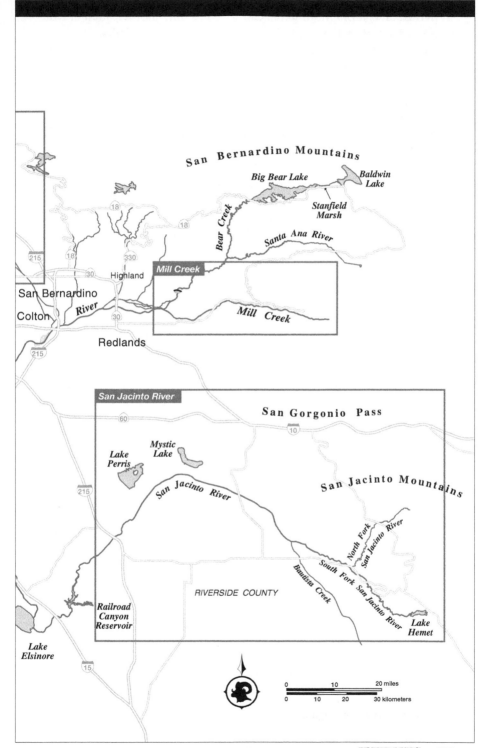

from the San Gabriel Mountains. Chino Creek and another, smaller Mill Creek carry waters that begin in and around the Chino Hills.

The San Jacinto River drains the mountain that shares the same name. Along its path to Lake Elsinore, it meets up with numerous smaller drainages. When Lake Elsinore fills, overflow waters join those shedding off the eastern slope of the Santa Ana Mountains and drain into Temescal Creek, which meets the Santa Ana River at Prado Dam.

The north slope of the Santa Ana Mountains sends water directly into the Santa Ana River from canyons like Coal and Gypsum. Carbon Creek overflow joins the river at the bottom of Santa Ana Canyon, but most of that creek's watershed actually drains into the San Gabriel River watershed.

In the heart of Orange County, the north half of the western slope of the Santa Ana Mountains feeds Santiago Creek through Fremont, Blackstar, Silverado, Modjeska, and Limestone canyons. Santiago Canyon is blocked at Irvine Lake and then again at Villa Park Dam before it gives way to the coastal plain where the creek then flows into the cities of Orange and Santa Ana before joining the Santa Ana River.

Because the Santa Ana River watershed is so broad and there are so many tributaries, a detailed description of each is not possible. For that reason, I have chosen to focus on a few of the tributaries that offer superior recreational opportunities or other points of interest that set them apart. This is not to say that these are the only tributaries that have recreational opportunities. In fact, with a little exploration, you can have a good time on most of the major tributaries to the Santa Ana River. Even the shortest tributaries that crisscross the higher elevations of the watershed offer a fine backdrop for an adventurous outing. So let this section be a starting point for your explorations of the tributaries of the Santa Ana River.

The tributaries described here begin in the upper watershed and then follow the watershed downstream.

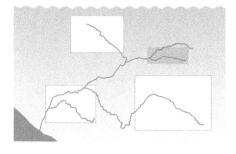

# MILL CREEK

Mill Creek is relatively short, but what it lacks in distance it makes up for in scenic beauty. The creek begins on the south side of the San Gorgonio Wilderness and quickly enters a steep, narrow canyon known as the Valley of the Falls—so named for the waterfalls that cascade off the sandstone cliffs and granite boulders of the canyon. Some people even go as far as to call this stream-cut valley a "little Yosemite."

Though the small communities of Forest Home and Forest Falls reside along Mill Creek, the area could hardly be considered developed. Property lines come right up to the edge of the trail to Big Falls, but there are few fences. Only scattered no-trespassing signs are in place to notify visitors of the boundaries.

After exiting the valley, Mill Creek spreads out over a wide, flat channel before meeting up with the Santa Ana River below Seven Oaks Dam. Though less scenic here, a carpet of wildflowers often blankets the Mill Creek floodplain during early spring or after summer rains.

Mill Creek has numerous primitive recreation opportunities and is a great choice for those wishing to enter the San Gorgonio Wilderness from lower elevations. The hardy hiker can do a multiday trip by beginning at the South Fork Trailhead and summiting San Gorgonio Mountain and then exiting via the Vivian Creek Trail to the valley floor. The really hardy might want to reverse the trip.

For those seeking a more casual experience, many short hikes and picnic locations can be found along Mill Creek. There are even several places where visitors can access the chilly grey-green water as it rushes toward the river. Mill Creek offers prime spots for swimming, fishing, or just lounging around.

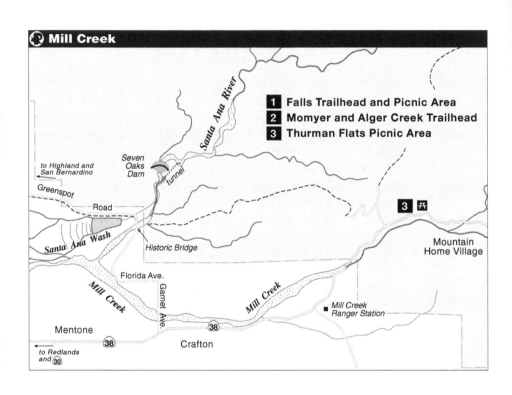

**Mill Creek**

**1** Falls Trailhead and Picnic Area
**2** Momyer and Alger Creek Trailhead
**3** Thurman Flats Picnic Area

*Santa Ana River*

*to Highland and San Bernardino*

Seven
Oaks
Dam

*tunnel*

Greenspot

Road

**3** 🏕

*Santa Ana Wash*

Historic Bridge

Mountain
Home Village

Florida Ave.

*Mill Creek*

*Mill Creek*

Garnet Ave.

■ *Mill Creek
Ranger Station*

Mentone

(38)

Crafton

(38)

*to Redlands
and* (30)

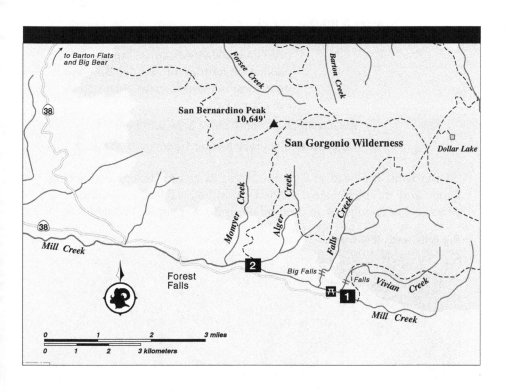

to Barton Flats
and Big Bear

Forsee Creek

Barton Creek

38

San Bernardino Peak
10,649'

San Gorgonio Wilderness

Dollar Lake

Momyer Creek

Alger Creek

Falls Creek

38

Mill Creek

Forest
Falls

2

Big Falls

Falls Vivian Creek

1

Mill Creek

0        1        2        3 miles
0    1    2    3 kilometers

# Falls Trailhead and Picnic Area

**HIGHLIGHTS:** Though this site gets a little crowded in summer, a mid-fall trip here provides solitude and opportunities for discovering some of Southern California's grandest waterfalls.

**ACCESS:** The Falls Trailhead is located at the east end of Valley of the Falls Drive, approximately 8 miles from the Mill Creek Ranger Station.

**SEASON & HOURS:** The picnic area is for day-use only (sunrise to sunset), however, those people holding overnight wilderness permits can use the parking lot for trips into the San Gorgonio Wilderness. All vehicles must display an Adventure Pass.

**FACILITIES:** Restrooms, picnic area, and trails.

**CONTACT:** Mill Creek Ranger Station: 909-382-2882.

At the Falls Trailhead and Picnic Area, there are dozens of parking spots, and the picnic area, shaded by incense-cedars and ponderosa pines, is big enough to accommodate up to 50 people. The tables here

**Big Falls feeds Mill Creek.**

are concrete and the retaining walls are made from local stone resembling the 1930s style commonly built by the Works Progress Administration throughout the watershed.

Once you leave the developed zone of pavement and concrete and enter Mill Creek, there's room for adventure. There is not a single, clearly defined trail; instead, numerous trails crisscross each other for some distance up and down the creek. The sign at the trailhead states that Big Falls is one-eighth of mile downstream, but it's easy to miss if you don't look closely because the falls are not on Mill Creek. Rather, they fall from a side canyon to the north.

This is a popular trailhead for accessing the San Gorgonio Wilderness via the Vivian Creek Trail. Some consider this route the most direct way to summit Southern California's highest peak, San Gorgonio Mountain. Whether or not you make it all the way to the top, it is a beautiful hike with stunning views almost immediately after you leave the trailhead.

# Momyer and Alger Creek Trailhead

**HIGHLIGHTS:** The views of Mill Creek Canyon and the relative lack of crowds make climbs on the Momyer and Alger Creek trails nice alternatives to the more crowded San Gorgonio Wilderness access routes.

**ACCESS:** The Momyer and Alger Creek Trailhead is a fairly large but nondescript parking area. From Hwy. 38, take Valley of the Falls Drive east for 3 miles. The trailhead is on the left (north), just downstream (west) of the Forest Service fire station.

**SEASON & HOURS:** Sunrise to sunset, and overnight parking is available for those staying in the wilderness area. All vehicles must display an Adventure Pass.

**FACILITIES:** Restroom, informational displays, and trails.

**CONTACT:** Mill Creek Ranger Station: 909-382-2882.

Momyer and Alger Creek trails provide great alternatives to the often crowded Vivian Creek Trail and north-side trails in the San Gorgonio Wilderness. Quiet campsites (Alger Creek Camp) with adequate and

**San Gorgonio Wilderness from the south**

dependable water can be found about 3.5 miles from the trailhead and then every mile or so thereafter to San Gorgonio Mountain. Tall pines and lush fern grottos form at springs and along year-round streams in this area. The great views here make even a short dayhike worthwhile.

The Momyer and Alger Creek Trailhead provides access to the San Gorgonio Wilderness via the Momyer and Alger Creek trails. This little-used access point also provides great views of the steep cliffs that form Mill Creek Canyon; look for the beautiful salt and pepper boulders that line Mill Creek in this area.

Momyer and Alger Creek trails are great crowd-free alternative routes into the San Gorgonio Wilderness. Though they do not provide very direct ascents to the peak, they do provide stunning views and excellent camping opportunities in the forest. The streams flow all year and there are several springs in the area that provide adequate water for overnight and extended explorations of the area.

# Thurman Flats Picnic Area

**HIGHLIGHTS:** The dense riparian forest that shelters the picnic area and the cool, crisp waters of Mill Creek make for a great summer escape without the long drive into the high country.

**ACCESS:** Thurman Flats can be accessed 2 miles east of the Mill Creek Ranger Station off of Hwy. 38.

**SEASON & HOURS:** Sunrise to sunset. An Adventure Pass is required here.

**FACILITIES:** Restrooms, interpretive displays, picnic area, and trails.

**CONTACT:** Mill Creek Ranger Station: 909-382-2882.

At the Thurman Flats Picnic Area, visitors can opt for a simple picnic at one of the tables shaded by oaks, or they can take one of the trails down to Mill Creek, where several large boulders along the water make nice lunch sites.

Interpretive signs at the parking area make for a worthwhile stop, even if you don't stay for a picnic. Short hikes down to the trail take you through a dense thicket of riparian vegetation rich with wildlife. Fishermen often ply the waters here, but some sections of the area may be closed seasonally to protect endangered toads and other amphibians.

**Thurman Flats stairs lead to Mill Creek.**

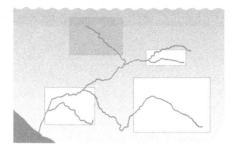

# LYTLE CREEK

Lytle Creek drains a portion of the San Gabriel Mountains, including Mt. Baldy, and it provides easy access for city-weary travelers seeking a quick getaway. There are actually three forks of Lytle Creek—the north, south, and middle forks—and each provides stunning scenery and excellent recreational opportunities.

The creek was named for Captain Andrew Lytle, who first camped here with a party of Mormon settlers in 1851. Captain Lytle stayed around for short time but eventually moved on, though his name commemorates his visit. Shortly after Lytle and his party set up camp at the mouth of the creek, someone found gold upstream and a mini gold rush was on. Although it never amounted to much, scars from that era can still be found along the slopes of Lytle Creek.

Today, the canyon is home to a small community known as Lytle Creek, which consists of three neighborhoods. It is hardly a city, but it is certainly much more developed than the area was when the Serrano Indians lived here.

In addition to the developed recreation opportunities described in this section, there are many other activities visitors can participate in throughout the Lytle Creek area. In particular, there are many primitive "yellow post" campsites along the middle and south forks of Lytle Creek. Check with the Forest Service for current conditions and availability. A fire swept through much of the Lytle Creek area in 2003, and several of the camp locations were engulfed by flames. At the time of this writing, little reparation had been made.

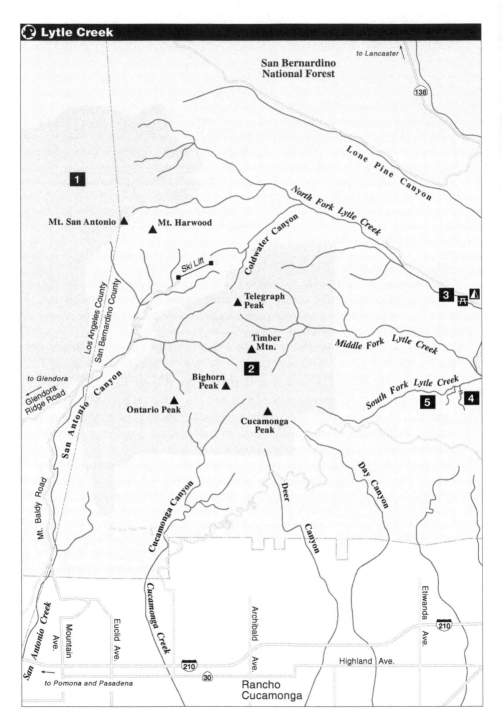

San Bernardino
National Forest

to Lancaster

138

**1**

Lone Pine Canyon

North Fork Lytle Creek

Mt. San Antonio ▲     Mt. Harwood ▲

Coldwater Canyon

Ski Lift

Telegraph
Peak ▲

**3** ⛩ ⚠

Timber
Mtn. ▲

Middle Fork Lytle Creek

Los Angeles County
San Bernardino County

**2**

to Glendora

Glendora
Ridge Road

San Antonio Canyon

Bighorn
Peak ▲

South Fork Lytle Creek

**5**     **4**

Ontario Peak ▲

Cucamonga
Peak ▲

Day Canyon

Mt. Baldy Road

Cucamonga Canyon

Deer Canyon

Canyon

Etiwanda Ave.

San Antonio Creek

Mountain Ave.

Euclid Ave.

Cucamonga Creek

Archibald Ave.

210

210

San

30

Highland Ave.

to Pomona and Pasadena

Rancho
Cucamonga

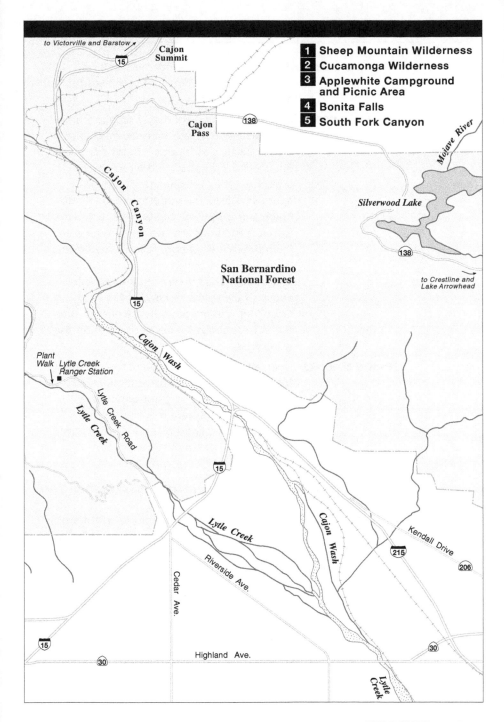

1 Sheep Mountain Wilderness
2 Cucamonga Wilderness
3 Applewhite Campground and Picnic Area
4 Bonita Falls
5 South Fork Canyon

to Victorville and Barstow
15
Cajon Summit
Cajon Pass
138

Mojave River

Silverwood Lake

138

San Bernardino National Forest

to Crestline and Lake Arrowhead

Cajon Canyon

15

Cajon Wash

Plant Walk
Lytle Creek Ranger Station

Lytle Creek Road

Lytle Creek

15

Lytle Creek

Cajon Wash

Kendall Drive

215
206

Riverside Ave.

Cedar Ave.

15
30
Highland Ave.
30
Lytle Creek

# Sheep Mountain Wilderness

**HIGHLIGHTS:** At Sheep Mountain Wilderness, you can watch sure-footed Big Horn Sheep scurry along rocky slopes.

**ACCESS:** Lytle Creek can be accessed from the Sierra Ave. exit on Interstate 15. Head north and follow Sierra, which turns into Lytle Creek Road. Follow the road to the recreation area. The Lytle Creek Ranger Station is approximately 2 miles north on Lytle Creek Road, and staff there can provide details on current conditions and activities in the area. From the ranger station, follow Lytle Creek Road, which becomes Forest Road 3N06. At Forest Road 3N33, turn right and drive for about 1 mile to the crossing of the Pacific Crest Trail. Parking pullouts are nearby. Hike the PCT for about 3 miles north to enter the wilderness.

**SEASON & HOURS:** Open all year, but be aware of the potential for cold, snowy conditions at higher elevations in winter and very hot summers. Wilderness permits are required for overnight stays, and Adventure Passes must be displayed in all parked cars.

**FACILITIES:** Trails.

**CONTACT:** Lytle Creek Ranger Station: 909-382-2851.

The 43,600-acre Sheep Mountain Wilderness ranges in elevation from 2100 to 10,064 feet at the summit of Mt. Baldy (also known as Mt. San Antonio), which is the highest point in the San Gabriel Mountains. The Sheep Mountain Wilderness is the headwaters for the North Fork of Lytle Creek.

John Muir referred to this area, which includes nearly 40 miles of trails, as some of the most rugged mountains he had explored. The range is so rugged that bighorn sheep still roam its rocky slopes. Mule deer, mountain lions, and black bears are also residents of the wilderness area. Also, keep your eyes open for some ancient limber pines that have grown in this wilderness area for centuries.

# Cucamonga Wilderness

**HIGHLIGHTS:** The wild and scenic character of the Middle Fork of Lytle Creek as it rushes from the Cucamonga Wilderness is one of the highlights of a trip into the area.

**ACCESS:** The Cucamonga Wilderness can be accessed from the Middle Fork Trailhead off of Middle Fork Road (Forest Road 2N58). From Lytle Creek Ranger Station, proceed north on Lytle Creek Road for about 1 mile. Turn left on Forest Road 2N58. Drive for approximately 4 miles and look for Stone House Camp and the Middle Fork Trailhead (parking available). Head west on the Middle Fork Trail, following the Middle Fork of Lytle Creek, and almost immediately enter the Cucamonga Wilderness.

Cucamonga Wilderness can also be accessed from the Mt. Baldy area by taking Interstate 10 to the Mountain Ave. exit and heading north on Mountain Ave. (which becomes Mt. Baldy Road). After about 15 miles, you will reach the Icehouse Canyon parking area. Take Icehouse Canyon Trail east into the wilderness.

**SEASON & HOURS:** Open all year, but be aware of hot temperatures in summer and cold temperatures and difficult conditions in winter. Wilderness permits are required for overnight stays and an Adventure Pass must be displayed in all parked cars.

**FACILITIES:** Trails.

**CONTACT:** Lytle Creek Ranger Station: 909-382-2851.

The Middle Fork of Lytle Creek as flows out of the Cucamonga Wilderness has been considered for wild and scenic designation, though it has not yet been granted. Nonetheless, anyone who visits the wilderness is sure to recognize the wild quality of this stretch of stream. It is forest-lined, cold, and fast. The stream appears to tumble in places as it maneuvers around large granite boulders.

Incense-cedars, ponderosa pine, and big-cone Douglas fir grace this wilderness area. Riparian woodlands line the Middle Fork as well as the smaller tributary drainages in the wilderness. Bighorn sheep, though less common than in the Sheep Mountain Wilderness, can be seen in the rugged landscape of the Cucamonga Wilderness.

# Applewhite Campground and Picnic Area

**HIGHLIGHTS:** The sounds of crackling campfires and a cascading creek sing campers to sleep in this not-so-far-away escape from the city.

**ACCESS:** The Applewhite Campground is located 3 miles north of the Lytle Creek Ranger Station on Lytle Creek Road.

**SEASON & HOURS:** Open all year. An Adventure Pass is required for use of the picnic area. Campsites cost $10 to $15, depending on the size of the site. Extra vehicles are $3 each.

**FACILITIES:** Restrooms, picnic areas, and camping.

**CONTACT:** Lytle Creek Ranger Station: 909-382-2851.

The Applewhite Campground is one of the least "natural" of the developed campsites in the San Bernardino National Forest. There is very little native vegetation within the campsites, but the campground is surrounded with chaparral and yellow pine habitat. Lytle Creek flows near enough that the sounds of the rushing stream can be heard once the crackle of campfire dies down.

**Applewhite Campground separates chaparral-covered slopes from the Lytle Creek Forest.**

**Applewhite Picnic Area is shaded by a riparian forest.**

Just across Lytle Creek Road from the Applewhite Campground is the Applewhite Picnic Area, which is restricted to day use but provides excellent access to Lytle Creek. The California Department of Fish and Game stocks Lytle Creek in this area with rainbow trout, and the location is a fly-fishing hot spot. The area is very popular in summer, but remains fairly quiet the rest of the year. An Adventure Pass is required for vehicular access to the Applewhite Picnic Area. A California fishing license is required for all fishing in the Lytle Creek area, except at private locations.

# Bonita Falls

**HIGHLIGHTS:** Watching water fall from high places always amazes spectators, and a trip to Bonita Falls is no exception.

**ACCESS:** Park in roadside turnouts just upstream of the Green Mountain Ranch sign about 1 mile north of the Lytle Creek Ranger Station on Lytle Creek Road.

**SEASON & HOURS:** Open for day use all year, weather permitting.

**FACILITIES:** None. The trail to Bonita Falls is unofficial and therefore is not maintained.

**CONTACT:** Lytle Creek Ranger Station: 909-382-2851.

To get to Bonita Falls from one of the parking areas, cross the creek and follow it upstream to the confluence of Lytle Creek and a small wash. Follow the wash for about a half mile upstream to the falls. The falls are not visible until you get very close to them.

This is not a developed site, and the trail is not part of the forest's managed trail system, so the trail is not regularly maintained; use it with caution.

Spring is the best time to view the falls and is also the nicest season to hike in this area, though any season can provide a nice experience. Check with the Lytle Creek Ranger Station for current conditions.

# South Fork Canyon

**HIGHLIGHTS:** Climbing over boulders and playing in the cold waters of the South Fork of Lytle Creek is worth the challenging access to this canyon.

**ACCESS:** The best access is via San Sevain Road, also called Big Tree Truck Trail on some maps. From Lytle Creek Road about 1 mile north of Interstate 15, head left (west) on Forest Road 1N34 for about 7 miles and look for small pullouts on either side of the road near the gate. If the gate is locked, continue up 1N34 on foot for another 2 miles to the crossing of the creek. If the gate is open, you can drive this last 2 miles to the old Joe Elliott Camp. Four-wheel drive vehicles are recommended. Call the Forest Service for current conditions and gate closures.

**SEASON & HOURS:** Open all year but can be extremely hot in summer and sometimes is closed due to fire danger. An Adventure Pass must be displayed in all parked cars.

**FACILITIES:** None.

**CONTACT:** Lytle Creek Ranger Station: 909-382-2851.

From the parking area, visitors can follow the creek and scramble up the canyon for at least 3 miles, though conditions may be extremely rugged and dangerous in places. The South Fork of Lytle Creek has cut a deep and rugged canyon through the hard granite of the San Gabriel Mountains. In some places, the creek drops steeply and is dangerous to descend. Ropes, helmets, and climbing harnesses are strongly recommended for this area.

As the creek reaches the canyon bottom, large rocks dot the area and make for fun and challenging bouldering. Visitors looking for a less challenging experience will find even the beginning of the canyon to be a pleasant experience, and the creek is always refreshing and enjoyable.

# SAN JACINTO RIVER

The San Jacinto River begins high in the San Jacinto Mountains where small streams combine to form north and south forks of the river. Mt. San Jacinto, Southern California's second highest peak, serves as the headwaters for both forks.

The North Fork of the San Jacinto River flows from the Mt. San Jacinto State Park, and the South Fork flows from the federally managed San Jacinto Wilderness Area south of the state park.

Numerous recreation opportunities abound along both forks. The Pacific Crest Trail crosses both forks, and many other trails in the area can easily be accessed from designated parking areas or by taking the Palm Springs Aerial Tramway to the park from the east side of the mountain range. Call 888-515-8726 or go to www.pstramway.com for current schedules and prices.

Although they are less common here than in the neighboring San Bernardino Mountains, black bears do roam the San Jacinto range. Bears are joined by mountain lions, bobcats, badgers, bighorn sheep, and many other small mammals and birds. They're gone now, but jaguars and grizzly bears once were residents of the range.

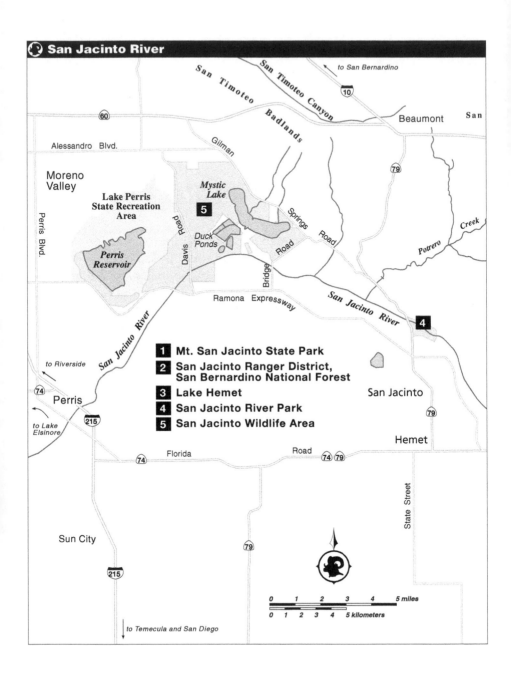

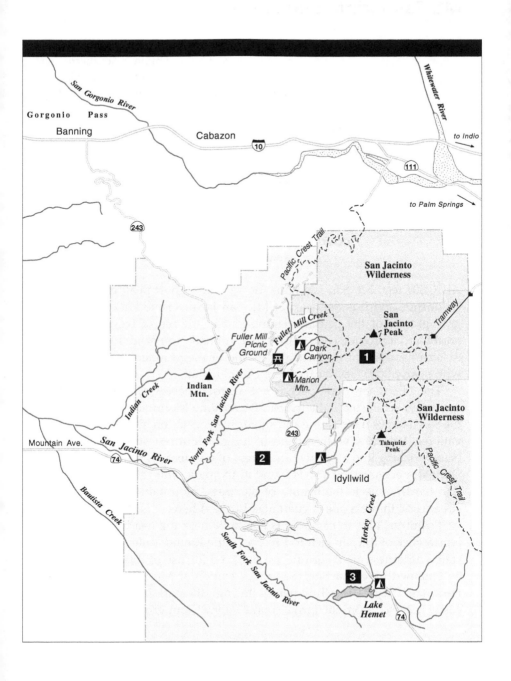

# Mt. San Jacinto State Park

**HIGHLIGHTS:** At Mt. San Jacinto State Park, you can visit the second highest mountain in Southern California. If you take the tramway, you'll cross many vegetation communities with little effort.

**ACCESS:** 25905 Hwy. 243, Idyllwild.

**SEASON & HOURS:** Sunrise to sunset. Overnight parking available with a state-issued wilderness permit, which is required for all multiday trips.

**FACILITIES:** Restrooms, picnic area, trails, camping, and nature center.

**CONTACT:** Mt. San Jacinto State Park: 951-659-2607; www.sanjac.statepark.org.

At 10,804 feet, Mt. San Jacinto is the second highest peak in Southern California, and it is the heart of Mt. San Jacinto State Park. The stark gray granite of the peak is reminiscent of the Sierra Nevada to the north, and it provides one of the most dramatic scenes in the state. The eastern escarpment in particular is one of the grandest in California, with nearly 9000 feet of exposed mountain wall.

The 14,000-acre state park is not all rock, however, as most of the mountain is forested. Like the San Bernardino Mountains to the north, the San Jacintos have alpine and subalpine vegetation in the highest elevations. A narrow vertical band of lodgepole forest stripes the range before turning into a yellow pine forest of ponderosa and Jeffrey pines. Some upper chaparral also is found in the park. This technical description hardly reflects the beauty of big trees, mountain meadows, and streamside thickets one is guaranteed to find here.

Primitive, hike-in camping is available near the headwaters of the North Fork of the San Jacinto River at Little Round Valley Camp in the state wilderness area. Permits are required for use of this site and can be obtained by contacting the ranger station at Mt. San Jacinto State Park. The Pacific Crest Trail passes through the park in this area and is easily accessed from the Little Round Valley Campground.

# San Jacinto Ranger District, San Bernardino National Forest

**HIGHLIGHTS:** The seamless management of state and federal lands makes visiting San Jacinto Mountain great for day trips or extended expeditions.

**ACCESS:** 54270 Pinecrest Road, Idyllwild.

**SEASON & HOURS:** Open all year, but it may be snowing in winter or crowded in summer. Campgrounds are available on a first-come, first-served basis or by reservation.

**FACILITIES:** Restrooms, picnic area, trails, and a visitor center.

**CONTACT:** San Jacinto Ranger District: 951-659-2607; campground reservations can be made at 877-444-6777.

The San Jacinto Ranger District of the San Bernardino National Forest is a high-country forest with recreational activities occurring at elevations of 5000 feet or higher. Numerous developed picnic areas and campgrounds can be found throughout the district, including Fern Basin, Marion Mountain, Black Mountain Group Camp, Lake Fullmer, and Apple Canyon. However, if you want to visit the San Jacinto River, head to Fuller Mill Creek Picnic Area and Dark Mountain Campground to access the North Fork.

Dark Mountain Campground (877-444-6777) is located at 7300 feet, making it a true high-country camp. The campground's 17 sites fill up fast, so be sure to reserve your spot in advance. Fishing, hiking, and wildlife-watching are great activities enjoyed from the Dark Mountain Campground.

Fuller Mill Creek Picnic Area is a developed picnic site located off Hwy. 243 approximately 8 miles northwest of the town of Idyllwild. The picnic tables here sit under a shaded canopy and restrooms are provided. The North Fork of the San Jacinto River, which runs nearby, harbors wild trout and Fuller Mill Creek is stocked regularly by California Fish and Game, making this area an angler's paradise.

# Lake Hemet

**HIGHLIGHTS:** Lake Hemet is the largest lake in the San Jacinto Mountains.

**ACCESS:** 56570 Hwy. 74, Mountain Center.

**SEASON & HOURS:** 6 AM to 10 PM in summer; 7 AM to 8 PM in winter.

**FACILITIES:** Restrooms, picnic area, camping, and a boat ramp.

**CONTACT:** Lake Hemet Water District: 951-659-2680; www.lakehemet.org.

Along the South Fork of the San Jacinto River, Lake Hemet provides opportunities for camping, picnicking, fishing, and boating. This year-round destination is managed by the Lake Hemet Water District to provide water for the San Jacinto Valley, including the cities of Hemet and San Jacinto.

There is a ramp for the small boats that are allowed on the lake; personal watercraft, such as jet skis, and other water contact, including swimming, are prohibited. Twelve-foot boats with 5-horsepower motors can be rented on a first-come, first-served basis. Kayaks and canoes are welcome on the waters of Lake Hemet.

Camping is available on a first-come, first-served basis. Electricity and sewer hookups are available at some sites. Camping is approximately $17 per night, but weekly and monthly rates are also available.

# San Jacinto River Park

**HIGHLIGHTS:** Relaxing in the shade of a mature cottonwood forest and soft sand of the river bottom is a great escape from the otherwise hot and dry desert.

**ACCESS:** The San Jacinto River Park is located where State Street, Saboba Road, and Gilman Springs Road all come together in the town of Gilman Hot Springs.

**SEASON & HOURS:** Day use (sunrise to sunset) of this area has been accepted, but overnight stays are frowned upon.

**FACILITIES:** None.

**CONTACT:** Riverside County Regional Parks and Open-Space District: 951-955-4310; www.riversidecountyparks.org.

This area is called out on several maps, including the *Rand McNally*, *Hemet*, and *Perris Road Map*. Although this area is not officially managed as parkland, it does see its share of recreational use and abuse. Activities range from bird-watching to illegal off-road vehicle and motorcycle races. This type of uncontrolled access has and will continue to take its toll on the river environment.

Currently, however, the channel, though mostly dry, is lined by a mature cottonwood forest and bordered by small willow groves. The slopes that rise above the river are covered with deer weed, sages, and buckwheat. This area represents the most mature riparian forest on the entire San Jacinto River.

**Mature cottonwoods are a sign of water in the desert.**

# San Jacinto Wildlife Area

**HIGHLIGHTS:** Bird songs to match the wide, open spaces make a trip to the San Jacinto Wildlife Area one visitors will never forget.

**ACCESS:** From the Ramona Expressway, take Davis Road north for 2 miles. The wildlife area is east of Lake Perris in unincorporated Riverside County.

**SEASON & HOURS:** Sunrise to sunset.

**FACILITIES:** Restrooms and trails.

**CONTACT:** San Jacinto Wildlife Area: 951-928-0580; www.dfg.ca.gov/lands/wa/region6/sanjacinto.html.

The San Jacinto Wildlife Area consists of approximately 4500 acres of land surrounding the historic channel of the San Jacinto River. The coastal sage scrub, grasslands, freshwater marsh, and riparian forest here form a landscape mosaic representing old California, with meadowlarks, red-winged blackbirds, and tri-colored blackbirds providing the soundtrack.

An auto tour introduces visitors to the various habitats and locations of the area, while several stops along it offer an opportunity for further exploration. Hunting is popular at the San Jacinto Wildlife Area, but check with the California Department of Fish and Game (951-928-0580; www.dfg.ca.gov/lands) for information about season and permits.

Wildlife at the site includes many waterfowl as well as shore and upland bird species. Mule deer, gray fox, coyote, and both of Southern California's remaining wild cat species, the bobcat and mountain lion, can be found here. Ring-tailed cats and skunks (striped and spotted) join a host of rodents in rounding out the species list.

One thing that makes the San Jacinto Wildlife Area unique is its use of reclaimed water in the habitat-restoration process. It was the first Fish and Game property to do so. The availability of water in the heat of summer ensures the success of the restoration effort while providing a reliable source of nourishment for the wildlife that has come to count on it.

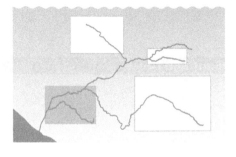

# SANTIAGO CREEK

Santiago Creek, one of the largest tributaries to the Santa Ana River and the largest within Orange County, begins at 5687 feet, at Santiago Peak, the higher of the two peaks that are commonly called Saddleback Mountain. Saddleback is the pinnacle of the Santa Ana Mountain range and it is the highest point in Orange County. Much of the Santa Anas are within the Trabuco Ranger District of the Cleveland National Forest, including the first several miles of Santiago Creek.

About 20 miles in length, this creek provides great opportunities for a natural or wild greenway in North Orange County. Much of its length is already bordered by parks, nature reserves, or public land. Numerous regional parks line the banks of the creek, and new ones are planned.

Trails parallel much of the creek. The Santiago Creek Bikeway begins in the city of Orange near the Grijalva Park and Sports Complex and it continues downstream into the city of Santa Ana, where it terminates next to the Discovery Science Center and Mainplace Mall. Future plans are to extend the bike trail upstream to Irvine Lake, where it will connect with trails leading into south Orange County and the future Great Park area. (This project is expected to be complete by 2010.) At the time of this writing, the city of Orange was beginning an effort to bring the trail to Santiago Oaks Regional Park. The county of Orange will then take up the effort carrying it to Irvine Lake.

The city of Santa Ana would like to connect the Santiago Creek Trail to the Santa Ana River Crest to Coast Trails, but it may not be able to keep the alignment in or next to the creek due to private property issues. (Some residents still believe that trails encourage crime, in spite of evidence to the contrary). The city will be able to connect to the river with a striped bike lane along 1.5 miles of road.

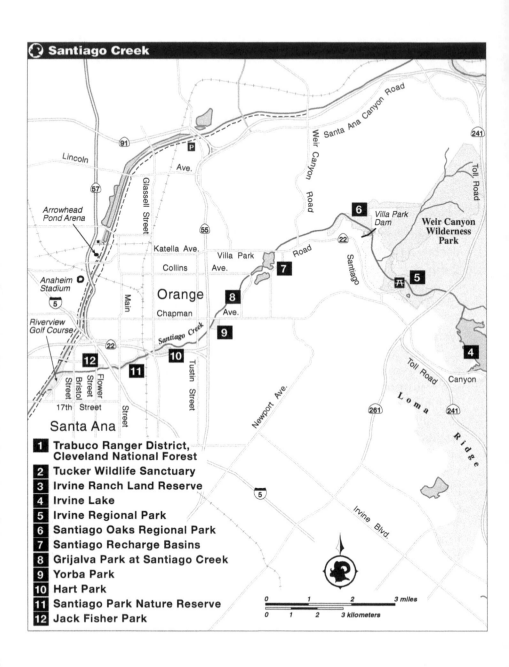

**Santa Ana Canyon Road**

241

Weir Canyon Road

Lincoln

91

Ave.

P

57

Glassell Street

Toll Road

**Arrowhead Pond Arena**

55

Weir Canyon Road

Road

**6** Villa Park Dam

**Weir Canyon Wilderness Park**

Katella Ave.

Villa Park

22

Collins Ave.

**7**

Santiago

☂ **5**

**Anaheim Stadium**

Main

**Orange**

**8**

5

Chapman Ave.

**Riverview Golf Course**

Santiago Creek

**9**

22

**10**

Toll Road

Canyon

**4**

**12**

Flower Street

Bristol Street

Street

**11**

Tustin Street

Newport Ave.

261

*L o m a*

241

17th Street

Street

**Santa Ana**

*R i d g e*

1 **Trabuco Ranger District, Cleveland National Forest**

2 **Tucker Wildlife Sanctuary**

3 **Irvine Ranch Land Reserve**

5

4 **Irvine Lake**

5 **Irvine Regional Park**

Irvine Blvd.

6 **Santiago Oaks Regional Park**

7 **Santiago Recharge Basins**

8 **Grijalva Park at Santiago Creek**

9 **Yorba Park**

10 **Hart Park**

11 **Santiago Park Nature Reserve**

0    1    2    3 miles

12 **Jack Fisher Park**

0    1    2    3 kilometers

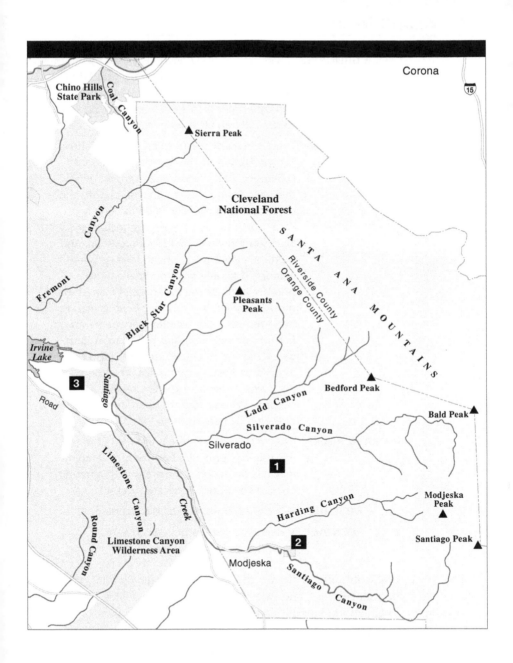

# Trabuco Ranger District, Cleveland National Forest

**HIGHLIGHTS:** A hike up Harding Canyon is worth the work in any season, but it is especially gratifying in spring when Humboldt lilies, seep orchids, and other rare plants are in bloom. Make it to the falls, and it even gets better.

**ACCESS:** There are many places to access the Trabuco Ranger District of the Cleveland National Forest, including a half-dozen truck trails that lead from Santiago Canyon up into the mountain high country (3000 to 5000 feet). From north to south, the roads include Blackstar Canyon Road, Silverado Road, and Modjeska Road (four-wheel-drive recommended if traveling beyond pavement). Additional roads can be accessed from these three. Seasonal closures may be in affect on these roads due to wildlife management and fire protection. Parking is provided at most gates and hiking and mountain biking often are allowed even when gates are closed. Call the Forest Service for current restrictions and closures. When gates are open, four-wheel-drive vehicles are recommended.

**SEASON & HOURS:** Open all year. Some areas are restricted to day use, but primitive backcountry camping may be allowed in some areas with a permit. Contact the Forest Service for details.

**FACILITIES:** Picnic area, trails, and a visitor center.

**CONTACT:** Trabuco Ranger District: 951-736-1811; www.fs.fed.us/r5/cleveland.

The Santa Ana Mountains make up the Trabuco Ranger District of the Cleveland National Forest, and about one third of the district drains into Santiago Creek via smaller creeks and canyons. This is a diverse landscape that at first glance appears to be a monoculture of chaparral, but for those who take the time to stop and get out of their cars, a wonderland awaits.

Canyon bottoms are filled with white alder, California sycamore, various willows, and coast live-oak. A few of these canyons have creeks with year-round flows, and the adventurer is likely to find a swimming hole or two with some effort and the better part of a day round trip.

Coastal sage scrub covers the lower slopes and is replaced by chaparral as the elevation increases. Coulter pine and big-cone Douglas fir can be found at upper elevations, and some old-growth stands in the forest even support spotted owls.

Nearly a dozen endemic species of plants can be found in the Santa Ana Mountains; a variety of matilija poppy is just one example. Numerous other rare and sensitive species make the range their home.

Though they are surrounded by millions of people, the Santa Anas still support wide-ranging predators. In fact, nearly two dozen mountain lions still cruise the range. The last grizzly bear in Southern California was killed in the Santa Ana Mountains in the early 1900s.

Most of the trails in the range eventually connect to the Main Divide Truck Trail, which follows the crest of the range. This trail leads south into San Diego County and north to the Santa Ana River and Chino Hills. The adventurer could, over three or four days, make a loop trip from the Santa Ana River, up Santiago Creek and then down the Main Divide and back to the Santa Ana River.

Though not in the Santiago Creek watershed, there are several campgrounds in the southern part of the Trabuco Ranger District, and all can be accessed from Hwy. 74. They are first-come, first-served camps, so check with the Trabuco Ranger District about availability prior to setting out.

**Centuries-old oaks dot the Trabuco Ranger District.**

# Tucker Wildlife Sanctuary

**HIGHLIGHTS:** Don't miss mornings on the viewing patio, especially during migration, when you're likely to encounter 20 or more bird species in one sitting.

**ACCESS:** 29322 Modjeska Canyon Road.

**SEASON & HOURS:** 7 AM to 5 PM.

**FACILITIES:** Restrooms, trails, and nature center.

**CONTACT:** Tucker Wildlife Sanctuary: 714-649-2760.

Tucker Wildlife Sanctuary, near the terminus of Modjeska Canyon Road, is a shining jewel in the necklace that is the quaint little community of Modjeska Canyon. The sanctuary, which is owned and managed by California State University, Fullerton, is popular on weekends, but overflow parking is available an eighth of a mile up (east) the road. Just beyond the first row of parking spots is a signed nature trail and observation patio that is connected to the caretaker's home. This small interpretive area also includes a pair of ponds and a small amphitheater. Santiago Creek runs seasonally through the area and can be viewed from a small pedestrian bridge that connects the patio to the trail.

On the opposite side of the road from the parking lot is a small interpretive center and the sanctuary office. Additional trails and habitat can be found surrounding the building, and a small picnic area and access to the national forest and Harding Canyon is just beyond the restrooms. The Braille Trail, a short nature trail with informational signs embossed in Braille, is to the east of the interpretive center.

**Tucker's tiny nature museum**

# Irvine Ranch Land Reserve

**HIGHLIGHTS:** Fremont Canyon Narrows and Dripping Springs in Limestone Canyon are just two of the many spectacular wild highlights within this reserve.

**ACCESS:** The reserve can be accessed from several points along Santiago Canyon Road, however, it is open only for guided tours and on a few open-access days. Reservations are required. Tours of the area are free, but call for a reservation and a schedule of tours and open-access days.

**SEASON & HOURS:** Day use by reservation only.

**FACILITIES:** Restrooms and trails.

**CONTACT:** The Irvine Ranch Land Reserve Trust: 714-508-4757; www.irvineranchlandreserve.org. The Nature Conservancy: 714-832-7478; www.nature.org.

This 45,000-acre reserve (described in detail on page 116) includes tributaries to Santiago Creek in Limestone Canyon and Fremont Canyon, two of the wildest, most diverse, and spectacular canyons in the region.

**Oak woodlands and coastal sage scrub are common on the Irvine Ranch Land Reserve.**

**Red rocks at the mouth of Blackstar Canyon highlight the geology of the Irvine Ranch Land Reserve.**

Limestone Canyon is famous for its stands of native California bunch-grass and unique geological formations. Fremont Canyon is rugged and relatively untouched by human development. The narrow, steep canyon even prevented cattle from getting very far, which has allowed the area to remain pristine.

Much of this land is part of the Central/Coastal Natural Communities Conservation Planning area, which was designed to protect large areas and a number of plant and animal species. The effort has had limited success; some of the target species have responded well, while others continue to decrease in number. In particular, large mammals such as the mountain lion have continued to suffer, and development in the area trudges along. Currently, a shoestring Nature Conservancy staff manages the land, and considering the circumstances, it has done a stellar job providing access while protecting the resources of the reserve.

# Irvine Lake

**HIGHLIGHTS:** Irvine Lake is the largest water body in the Santa Ana Mountains and provides spectacular views and a sense of solitude that often only come from being on the water.

**ACCESS:** 4621 Santiago Canyon Road, Orange.

**SEASON & HOURS:** Fishing-only visitors can enter from 6 AM to 4 PM. Gates open at 8 AM on Friday and Saturday for camping.

**FACILITIES:** Restrooms, camping, store, café, boat ramp, and boat rentals.

**CONTACT:** Irvine Lake: 714-649-9111; www.irvinelake.net.

Irvine Lake is a reservoir originally created to provide water for ranching and farming operations on the Irvine Ranch, but now it provides water for the growing communities of East Orange. It also has recreational opportunities, including a private fishing operation, camping along the shore of the 700-acre lake, a café, and a tackle shop. Small fishing boats are allowed and can be rented from the store. The lake is a great place to watch birds, fish for record-sized trout, and view the remarkable landscape of the Santa Ana Mountains. In addition to the fish stocked in the lake, a small population of the endangered three-spine stickleback also inhabits the water of Irvine Lake.

**Irvine Lake is the largest water body in the Santa Ana Mountains.**

# Irvine Regional Park

**HIGHLIGHTS:** Ride along the meandering trails of California's oldest regional park.

**ACCESS:** 1 Irvine Park Road, Orange.

**SEASON & HOURS:** Winter, 7 AM to 6 PM; summer, 7 AM to 9 PM. There is a $4 vehicle entrance fee.

**FACILITIES:** Restrooms, picnic sites, train rides, horse rentals, pedal-boat rentals, zoo, nature center, and trails.

**CONTACT:** Irvine Regional Park: 714-973-6835; www.ocparks.com/irvine.

Irvine Regional Park has the distinction of being the first regional park in California. James Irvine Sr., an Orange County ranching pioneer, donated the first 160 acres to the county of Orange in 1876, and the park has since grown to 477 acres. Today, it is one of the most popular parks in the county system.

Irvine Park, as it is best known, is a mixed-use park with ball fields, picnic sites, and natural wilderness areas. The park also hosts several concessions, including a train, horseback riding, and pedal-boat rentals. The miles of trails winding through the park lead to some of the ridgelines offering tremendous views of the Orange County coastal plain.

**Irvine is California's first regional park.**

**Classic nature center style at Irvine Park**

Great dayhikes and casual mountain bike rides can be staged from the park, which also provides easy access to Santiago Creek from the north and east ends of the park. The park also offers a relaxing environment for quick lunches or daylong picnics. On holidays, the park often fills to capacity by 10 AM, closing to additional visitors afterward, so be sure to get there early on popular days.

# Santiago Oaks Regional Park

**HIGHLIGHTS:** On late spring evenings, you can listen to the chorus of frogs along the riparian forest that lines Santiago Creek as it flows through the park.

**ACCESS:** 2145 Windes Drive, Orange.

**SEASON & HOURS:** 7 AM to sunset. The park closes for three days following significant rainfall.

**FACILITIES:** Restrooms, picnic area, trails, and watershed interpretive center.

**CONTACT:** Santiago Oaks Regional Park: 714-973-6620; www.ocparks.com/santiagooaks.

Santiago Oaks Regional Park is actually three separate parcels all within the Santiago Creek watershed. The park ranges from shady oak groves and riparian woodlands to coastal sage scrub vegetation communities. Even a historic orange grove is preserved in the heart of the park.

**An oak-covered trail leads to Santiago Creek at Santiago Oaks Regional Park.**

Just like at its sister park, Irvine Regional, Santiago Creek runs through the middle of Santiago Oaks Regional Park. There is even a historic agriculture-era dam preserved within the park, as well as access to the Villa Park Dam, a larger, more modern earthen dam that provides flood protection for the communities below.

Santiago Oaks is popular with equestrians, hikers, and mountain bikers. Many of the homes that surround the park are horse properties, and Santiago Oaks provides a place to trail ride. Some equestrians trailer in their horses.

The park can be rented for weddings and other special events, but it is school children who comprise one of the largest visitor groups. A watershed center is one of the attractions at the park and many school children visit the center on fieldtrips.

# Santiago Recharge Basins

**HIGHLIGHTS:** Stunning views across one of Orange County's largest water bodies make the "Santiago Pits" a highlight of any trip to Santiago Creek.

**ACCESS:** The pits are bordered by Hewes Ave. on the east, Prospect Ave. on the west, Bond Street on the south, and Katella Ave. on the north. Entrance to the pits is forbidden except by permission from the Orange County Water District; however, you can follow a trail or the sidewalks that surround the pits.

**SEASON & HOURS:** Pits are open by reservation only. Public sidewalks and trails surrounding the pits and are always open.

**FACILITIES:** None.

**CONTACT:** Orange County Water District: 714-378-3206; www.ocwd.com.

The Santiago Recharge Basins are former sand and gravel pits mined during the 1960s and '70s. The steep walls and porous material provide excellent opportunities to percolate water back into the massive Orange

**The "Santiago Pits" offer great views down Santiago Creek.**

County groundwater basin. Today, there is little more to do than view the lakes and the many birds and wildlife that use it, however, a trail is planned to provide bike riding and pedestrian access around the large bodies of water.

Today, the Orange County Water District pumps water from the Santa Ana River to fill the Santiago Basins and release some water down the creek to increase its recharge capabilities. Though there is little public access to the area, the basins form large lakes in the middle of an otherwise developed area and add to the beauty of Santiago Creek.

# Grijalva Park at Santiago Creek

**HIGHLIGHTS:** A willow woodland lines Santiago Creek at Grijalva Park's western edge and makes for a great shady summer getaway.

**ACCESS:** 368 North Prospect Ave., Orange.

**SEASON & HOURS:** 7 AM to 9 PM.

**FACILITIES:** Restrooms, sports fields, playground, and trails.

**CONTACT:** City of Orange Parks Department: 714-744-7274; www.cityoforange.org/depts/commserv.

Development of Grijalva Park began in 2000, and at the time of this writing, it was only half built. The park is mostly turf that serves as soccer fields, with a small area dedicated to native plants. A small public building anchors the east end of the park, while Santiago Creek makes up the western border.

When complete around 2010, the park will include a public swimming pool, gymnasium, and, advocates hope, areas where Santiago Creek has been enhanced and the native vegetation restored. The Santiago Creek Bike Trail passes through Grijalva Park, and numerous footpaths parallel the creek. Some of the best habitat along the creek is found at the edge of the park. The park is named for the first European settler in Orange County and the founder of the Rancho Santiago de Santa Ana.

**Grijalva is Orange's newest park.**

# Yorba Park

**HIGHLIGHTS:** Yorba Park is one of the last large open-space areas on lower Santiago Creek and provides many recreational opportunities, including a dog park.

**ACCESS:** 190 South Yorba Street, Orange.

**SEASON & HOURS:** 7 AM to 9 PM.

**FACILITIES:** Restrooms and a dog park.

**CONTACT:** City of Orange Parks Department: 714-744-7274; www.cityoforange.org/depts/commserv.

Yorba Park is the most popular unwanted park in the city of Orange. The city has been threatening to sell Yorba Park for several years, claiming its development and maintenance costs are too high because of its previous incarnation as a landfill. However, the city has been unsuccessful in convincing any of the thousands of people that use it every month. In fact, a recent community-driven effort was successful at developing a 2-acre dog park in a portion of the "unusable" Yorba Park.

Regardless of the politics that surround Yorba, the creekside open space is nice and has the potential to become the best-used park in the city, especially when the bike trail connects and the city opens the gates.

**Yorba Park is home to Orange's only dog park.**

# Hart Park

**HIGHLIGHTS:** Hart Park is a very nice spot, and the east end of the park, where developed recreation gives way to the wild side of lower Santiago Creek, is not to be missed.

**ACCESS:** 701 South Grand Street, Orange. In addition to the main entrance on Grand, there are entrances at 700 South Shaffer Ave. and 701 South Glassell Street.

**SEASON & HOURS:** 7 AM to 9 PM.

**FACILITIES:** Restrooms, playgrounds, picnic area, trails, and sports fields.

**CONTACT:** City of Orange Parks Department: 714-744-7274; www.cityoforange.org/depts/commserv.

Construction on Hart Park, the oldest park in the city of Orange, was mostly completed in the 1930s as part of the Works Progress Administration's local efforts; however, portions of the park predate that work by decades, and much has been added since then. Today, the park includes a swimming pool known to locals as "the plunge," several ball diamonds, and numerous picnic areas.

Like it does at many parks described in this section, Santiago Creek runs right through the middle of this park. However, unlike at the other parks, the creek through Hart Park is literally a parking lot. Negotiations are underway between the city of Orange and Orange County Water District to provide a low-flow mechanism that will allow recharge waters to pass through the park without causing a loss of parking.

Hart Park has been at the center of the community since its establishment, and it continues in that function today. Orange High School holds all of its reunions here. Pancake breakfasts, classic car shows, creek cleanups, and summer concerts all take place in the park.

# Santiago Park Nature Reserve

**HIGHLIGHTS:** At Santiago Park Nature Reserve, you can find wilderness in the heart of the city.

**ACCESS:** Santiago Park is 1.25 miles long and can be accessed from 2535 North Main Street and 510 East Memory Lane. Access the nature reserve at 900 East Memory Lane.

**SEASON & HOURS:** The nature reserve is open from 7 AM to sunset and evenings by reservation. The remainder of Santiago Park is open from 7 AM to 9 PM.

**FACILITIES:** Restrooms, playgrounds, picnic area, trails, sport fields, and tennis court.

**CONTACT:** Santiago Park Nature Reserve: 714-571-4288; www.ci.santa-ana.ca.us/parks.

Santiago Park Nature Reserve is the city of Santa Ana's first nature reserve, founded in 2001, although it has been parkland since 1935 and it remains a work in progress. However, the reserve is beautiful, with mature coast live-oak woodlands mixing with riparian woodlands and coastal sage scrub filling in the sunny pockets of this 18-acre urban natural area.

**Orange County Conservation Corps members take a break in the shade of oaks at Santiago Park Nature Reserve.**

At the time of writing, plans were being finalized for a small interpretive center and native meadow or grassland. When complete in 2008, 10,000 school children a year will tour through the park to experience nature in their own backyards.

Santiago Creek Bike Trail meanders through the park and nature reserve, and an additional 1.5 miles of running, hiking, biking, and equestrian trail accompany it. Several interpretive areas can be found along the trails and any visit to the park will be an educational experience.

However, not all of the park has wilderness characteristics. There are also playgrounds, picnic sites, a ball diamond, tennis courts, and lawn bowling greens. The Discovery Science Center borders the west end of the park and can be accessed from the Santiago Creek Bike Trail. The science center provides hands-on educational experiences in physics and technology.

# Jack Fisher Park

**HIGHLIGHTS:** Nearly a century old, Jack Fisher Park has a very historic feel, making it a nice stop along Santiago Creek.

**ACCESS:** 2501 North Flower Street, Santa Ana.

**SEASON & HOURS:** 7 AM to 9 PM.

**FACILITIES:** Restrooms, playground, and picnic area.

**CONTACT:** Santa Ana Parks, Recreation, and Community Services Agency: 714-571-4200; www.ci.santa-ana.ca.us/parks.

This tiny park is the second oldest in Orange County's oldest city and it is the final park along Santiago Creek before the creek empties into the Santa Ana River. It borders Santiago Creek and has historic stairways that lead right into the creek. A playground, restrooms, and picnic site are available, and a log cabin here can be rented for private events.

**Jack Fisher Park is one of the oldest city parks in Orange County.**

# HISTORICAL SITES
# AND CULTURAL
# RESOURCES

The Santa Ana is the oldest river in Southern California and is rich with history. Visitors to her watershed can uncover the past at every bend of the river and in every community along its banks. This chapter highlights some of these sites.

Some of these sites are no more than a historic marker or sign describing what happened there centuries earlier. Others are preserved in all of their original prosperity. These sites are described in order of their occurrence in the watershed, beginning in the headwaters and heading downstream. Most are directly related to the river, though some have a greater connection than others. There are many more historically important sites in the Santa Ana River watershed, but the sites described here are fairly close to the river and are easy to access.

One notable absence in the historical timeline of the sites described here is Native American places. The sites described here are maintained or managed and the land use around them is monitored. This is not the case of most indigenous sites in the watershed and vandalism and poaching of artifacts continues to be a problem. In addition, the native people who lived within the Santa Ana River watershed considered all lands sacred and did not build permanent structures to be left behind as they moved on. Individual plants or gathering areas were of great importance to the tribes, and their ceremonial sites were adorned with sand paintings designed to be carried away by the spirit of the wind.

*left:* **Mural at the Asistencia Museum**

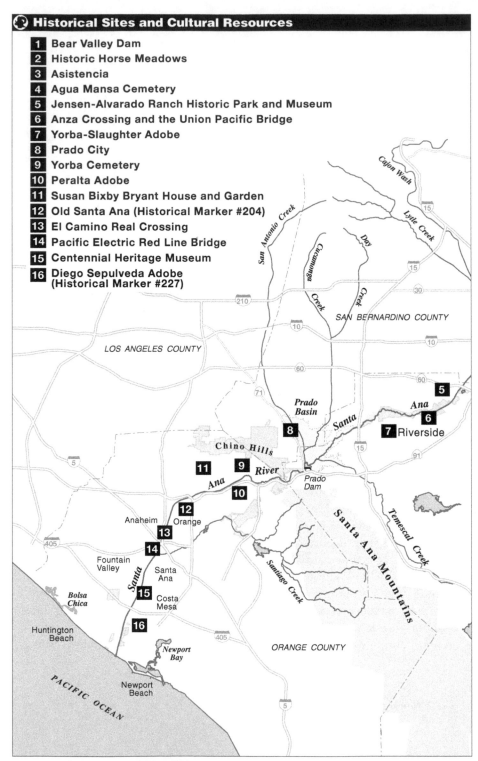

## Historical Sites and Cultural Resources

1. Bear Valley Dam
2. Historic Horse Meadows
3. Asistencia
4. Agua Mansa Cemetery
5. Jensen-Alvarado Ranch Historic Park and Museum
6. Anza Crossing and the Union Pacific Bridge
7. Yorba-Slaughter Adobe
8. Prado City
9. Yorba Cemetery
10. Peralta Adobe
11. Susan Bixby Bryant House and Garden
12. Old Santa Ana (Historical Marker #204)
13. El Camino Real Crossing
14. Pacific Electric Red Line Bridge
15. Centennial Heritage Museum
16. Diego Sepulveda Adobe (Historical Marker #227)

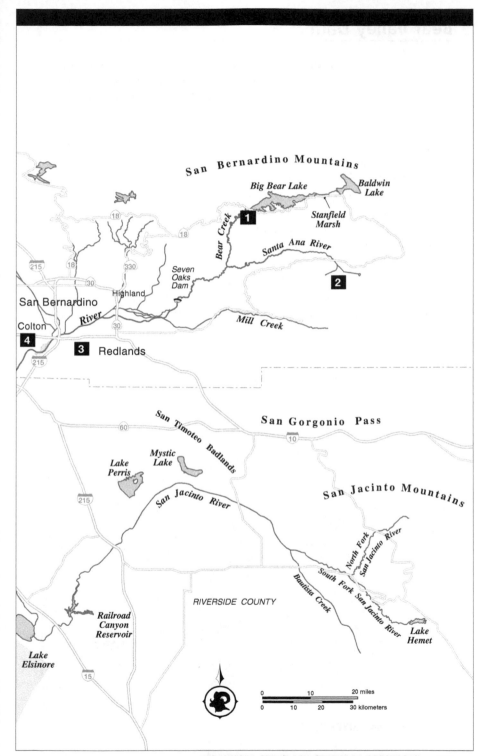

San Bernardino Mountains

Big Bear Lake

Baldwin Lake

Stanfield Marsh

**1**

Bear Creek

Santa Ana River

**2**

Seven Oaks Dam

Highland

San Bernardino

River

Colton

**4**

**3** Redlands

San Timoteo Badlands

San Gorgonio Pass

Mystic Lake

Lake Perris

San Jacinto Mountains

San Jacinto River

North Fork San Jacinto River

South Fork San Jacinto River

Bautista Creek

RIVERSIDE COUNTY

Railroad Canyon Reservoir

Lake Hemet

Lake Elsinore

0    10    20 miles
0    10    20    30 kilometers

# Bear Valley Dam

**ACCESS:** Bear Valley Dam can be found at the west end of Big Bear Lake, at intersection of highways 18 and 38, 5 miles west of Big Bear Village.

Originally built in 1894 as a single arch structure, the Bear Valley Dam was constructed to provide water for irrigation in Redlands. The original reservoir held 25,000 acre feet of water, but after several years of above average precipitation, planners decided a bigger water supply was warranted. In 1912, a new, larger dam was completed that increased the reservoir to more than 73,000 acre feet.

The original dam still stands, but it is under water in all but the driest of times. The new dam stands 100 yards downstream of the original. A small parking area and historic plaque are located on the south end of the lake, just east of the dam. This is a popular fishing site and provides amazing views of both the lake and valley as well as down Bear Creek Canyon.

**This marker commemorates both Bear Valley Dams.**

# Historic Horse Meadows

**ACCESS:** Historic Horse Meadows can be accessed only by taking the South Fork Trail 2 miles up from the South Fork Trailhead parking area on Jenks Lake Road. To reach the trailhead, take Hwy. 38 to Jenks Lake Road and turn south. Follow Jenks Lake Road for 2 or 3 miles (3 miles from Jenks Lake Road west and 2 miles from Jenks Lake Road east) to the parking area on the north side of the road.

Historic Horse Meadows is an open, serene, tree-lined meadow at just below 7500 feet. Depart from the parking lot and follow the trail immediately across the road from the restrooms. Cross the dirt road at about 0.75 mile and stay on the trail. In just about another mile up the hill, the trail levels out and Horse Meadows is on the left side of the trail.

In its heyday, the area, including the two small cabins and corrals, would have housed a half dozen horses and nearly as many rangers. The facility was a backcountry outpost for rangers conducting timber surveys and patrolling forest lands in the era preceding the automobile. The outpost was retired as a full-time station in the 1950s.

Today, Horse Meadows is the last human "works" before the San Gorgonio Wilderness, and it is a fairly easy 750-foot elevation gain from the parking area. Just beyond Horse Meadows and its picnic tables is Poop Out Hill, named for the many who turn back before reaching the summit of this rise.

Surrounded by tall pine and fir trees, Horse Meadows is a natural wet meadow covered with stiff bunch grasses, sedges, and wildflowers in spring. The two small cabins are open, and interpretive signs and historic photos grace the walls. Today, evidence of horses is limited to a falling-down pipe corral behind the cabins.

# Asistencia

**ACCESS:** 26930 Barton Road, Redlands; 909-793-5402.

Originally built around 1819 about a mile from its current location, Asistencia was an outpost of the Mission San Gabriel. At that time, it was merely a small chapel surrounded by a low wall and was used to serve Mass.

In 1830, the Asistencia or "Estancia" was relocated to its present site, and a major complex was constructed, beginning with a 14-room adobe building. Four years later, the facility was all but abandoned when the missions were stripped of their land and power by Mexican decree.

The Lugo Brothers, Jose del Carmen, Vicente, and Jose Maria, with their cousin Diego Sepulveda, were granted the Rancho San Bernardino, which included the Asistencia in 1843. They sold the rancho less than 10 years later to a group of Mormon settlers.

The Mormons began agricultural and manufacturing operations around the site using water from the Indian-built Zanja, a canal that brought water for irrigation from the Santa Ana River. Just five years after moving onto the land, the Mormons sold the Asistencia and surrounding property.

**The Asistencia is a San Gabriel Mission outpost.**

Dr. Ben Barton, for whom Barton Road and presumably Barton Flats in the San Bernardino Mountains were named, moved into the facility in 1859. He stayed on the property for the next 25 years, but he built a new residence and let the older adobe fall into ruin.

The facility was artistically restored by 1937 using skills and labor of the Works Progress Administration. In 1960, it was dedicated as a historic landmark and today is operated by the San Bernardino Museum.

# Agua Mansa Cemetery

**ACCESS**: 2001 W. Agua Mansa Road, Colton; 909-370-2091. Open the first Sunday of every month or by appointment.

Agua Mansa Cemetery is all that's left of the two small 1850s settlements along the Santa Ana River called La Placita and Agua Mansa. Together, known as San Salvador, they were prosperous farming communities until the flood of 1862. In that year, a wall of water flowed from the mountains, washing the communities away. Only a few buildings on the bluff and the cemetery survived.

Prior to the flood, farming, lumber, and other community activities occurred here. In 1978, a replica of the original San Salvador Chapel was built on the cemetery grounds and now serves as a museum and store.

**The remains of La Placita and Agua Mansa**

# Jensen-Alvarado Ranch Historic Park and Museum

> **ACCESS:** 4307 Briggs Street, Riverside; 951-369-6055. Open to the public Saturdays, 10 AM to 4 PM. School and group tours can be scheduled daily. Call for a schedule of special events, including summer camp, July Fourth celebration, and Ranch Days.

This 32-acre park is worth the visit for anyone interested in historic California. Originally constructed in 1868 as the headquarters for the Jensen-Alvarado Ranch, the series of brick buildings are some of the first such structures in Southern California. The bricks were made of clay mined on the Jensen Ranch not far from the existing buildings.

A brick winery was built shortly after the home was constructed, and it is equal in size to the living quarters. The winery now serves as a museum, and the entire facility has a wonderful atmosphere and cheerful and knowledgeable staff. Additional historic structures, live ranch animals, and interpretive signs can be found throughout the grounds.

**One of California's first clay brick buildings**

# Anza Crossing and the Union Pacific Bridge

**ACCESS:** Located between Martha McLean-Anza Narrows Regional Park (at 5759 Jurupa Ave.) and Jurupa Hills Country Club (6161 Moraga Ave.), Riverside. The best access to the site is within the park.

While Americans were fighting the Revolutionary War on the East Coast of North America, Juan Bautista de Anza was leading cattle, horses, and a handful of hardy settlers across the West on the first overland route to the California coast. On January 1, 1776, the party crossed the Santa Ana River where, today, parks and golf courses can be found.

This site proved to be such an optimal river crossing that a century and a half later, the Union Pacific Railroad built a multi-arched bridge across the river. The massive bridge still stands and is in daily use. Historic markers can be found in both Martha McLean-Anza Narrows Regional Park and Jurupa Hills Country Club.

**The historic Union Pacific Bridge is architecturally unique and attractive.**

# Yorba-Slaughter Adobe

**ACCESS:** 17127 Pomona Rincon Road, Corona. Open Wednesday through Saturday, 10 AM to 5 PM. Yorba-Slaughter Adobe is a facility of the San Bernardino County Museum: 909-307-2669.

The Yorba-Slaughter Adobe is not your typical adobe structure: It's large, has a porch that circles the entire house, and there are doors and windows all around the house. There's also no fireplace. In fact, about the only thing that makes this house similar to other adobes is the mud brick it is built with.

This adobe building was built in 1852 after an earlier home burned down. It is the oldest existing structure in San Bernardino County and was occupied until 1918 and then vacant until 1929 when restoration began. The property was named "Buena Vista" by Raimundo Yorba, who inherited the Rancho Santiago de Santa Ana and purchased 18,000 additional acres from the Bandini Ranch. The adobe was an important part of the town of Rincon, later called Prado City. It likely served as the post office and was a stop on the Butterfield Stage Route.

Buena Vista was purchased in 1868 by Fenton Slaughter, a veteran of the Mexican War and a successful sheep and cattle rancher. During his time at Buena Vista, Slaughter was in the state assembly and was a San Bernardino County supervisor for five years.

**The Vine Slope Winery at the Yorba-Slaughter Adobe**

# Prado City

ACCESS: Euclid Ave. and Hwy. 71.

Most of the town of Prado, or Rincon as it was called in the late 1800s, is submerged by the waters behind Prado Dam. Today, only a few structures remain above the waterline, including the Yorba-Slaughter Adobe described on page 212. A small cemetery is located in the Prado Basin Recreation Area and much of the past of Prado can be seen in pictures at the Prado Dam Interpretive Center (951-898-6169) and other museums and libraries in the region.

# Yorba Cemetery

ACCESS: Woodgate Park, Yorba Linda, Open the first Saturday of every month from 11:30 AM to 12:30 PM. Call for tour reservations and directions: 714-973-3190.

Yorba Cemetery was deeded by Don Bernardo Yorba to the Catholic Church in 1858. Built in 1850, the small private cemetery is the second oldest in Orange County, predated only by the mission cemetery in San Juan Capistrano.

**Gateway to the graves at Yorba Cemetery**

Yorba Cemetery closed in 1939, but when it was open it became the final resting place famous historic Californians, with names like Yorba, Serrano, and Peralta.

# Peralta Adobe

**ACCESS:** 6398 Santa Ana Canyon Road, Anaheim, 714-973-3190. Open the first Saturday of the month, from 10 AM to 11 AM.

The Peralta Adobe was originally constructed by Ramon Peralta in 1871 and restored more than 100 years later in 1985. Though it was not the only adobe built in the Rancho Santiago de Santa Ana, it is the best preserved one and the only one left in Santa Ana Canyon. The small, square, single-story building is now surrounded on three sides by a Tarbell Realty office that has been designed to mimic the original structure. The building is on the corner of Santa Ana Canyon Road and Fairmont Blvd., on the edge of a retail center. Interpretive exhibits are located inside the building.

# Susan Bixby Bryant House and Garden

**ACCESS:** 5700 Susanna Bryant Drive, Yorba Linda. Open for house and garden tours on Sunday from 1 PM to 4 PM or by reservation. A donation is required to enter.

The Bixby ranch was carved from the original Rancho Canon de Santa Ana through purchase from Bernardo Yorba. In 1911, following John Bixby's death, Susanna Bixby Bryant took over the ranch operations. The ranch house that stands today was built for Susanna shortly after she took the reins of the business. It was fully restored in 1997 and now serves as a museum.

In 1927, the original Rancho Santa Ana Botanical Garden was established on the land surrounding the house, which overlooks the Santa Ana River. The garden is recognized today as a leader in botanical preservation and research. It was moved to Claremont College in 1951, but a small assemblage of native specimens still grace the grounds of the historic home.

Susanna Bixby Bryant died in 1946 and the ranch was developed into the residential communities of Yorba Linda between 1978 and 1985.

# Old Santa Ana (Historical Marker #204)

**ACCESS:** Northwest corner of Lincoln Ave. and Orange-Olive Road, Orange.

On this site, in the first half of the 19th century, a small town alongside the Santa Ana River bustled with activity. The original town of Santa Ana was at the heart of the Rancho Santiago de Santa Ana and had an elected mayor, a general store, and hotel. Then, in 1862, the Santa Ana River changed course and moved away from the town. Eventually, the cities of Orange and (new) Santa Ana grew to overshadow the smaller village to the north, and the site was abandoned. Today, only a historical marker is left to call attention to the site, and even the river has forgotten about the site.

**This plaque marks the original site of Santa Ana.**

# El Camino Real Crossing

**ACCESS:** Chapman Ave. crossing of the Santa Ana River, Orange.

The bridge here today is modern and no sign or monument exists now, but prior to the 1950s, this river crossing was considered one of the most important. It was one of the first permanent bridges across the river and was the location where Juan Gaspar de Portola and Father Junipero Serra crossed the river, dubbing the route "El Camino Real," or the King's Road. It later became Hwy. 101, which connected San Diego to Los Angeles. Known today as Chapman Ave., it remains an important river crossing.


# Pacific Electric Red Line Bridge

**ACCESS:** One-quarter mile north of 5th Street, Santa Ana. Access this bridge by parking at Spurgeon School and walking north on the Santa Ana River Trail.

The Pacific Electric Railroad was a commuter rail line in the early 1900s that not only rivaled but exceeded today's Metrolink service. Dozens of lines ran throughout Southern California and served millions of passengers annually. The Santa Ana/Los Angeles Line began service in

**The Pacific Electric Bridge Red Line connects miles of potential trails.**

1903 and ran the full length until 1950. Portions of the line continued until 1958. Known as the Red Cars or Red Line, the service hit its peak in 1945 when it carried more than 2.5 million passengers on the Santa Ana Line alone. Eventually, the line was outdone by Southern California's fascination with the automobile.

All that is left locally of the Santa Ana to Los Angeles Line is much of the right-of-way and this historic bridge, built around 1904. For decades, trail advocates have wanted to open this dirt path that connects the Santa Ana River to the San Gabriel River. Light rail and transit advocates also see potential in the route. Today, however, it sits vacant, begging the imagination of those who pass.

# Centennial Heritage Museum

**ACCESS:** 3101 West Harvard Street, Santa Ana (next to Centennial Regional Park), 714-540-0404. Open Wednesday through Friday, 1 to 5 PM. Entrance into the historic homes on the museum grounds is $5 per person, but the grounds can be toured for free.

Centennial Heritage Museum (formerly Discovery Museum of Orange County) is a 9-acre historic park that showcases elements of Orange County's history that includes indigenous culture through the 1890s agricultural period. Approximately 5 acres of the site are natural, and

**Centennial Hill is the highest point in Santa Ana.**

**Home of Hiram Clay Kellogg, who first attempted to tame the Santa Ana River**

ecological restoration is in progress. Santa Ana's only remaining freshwater marsh occurs on this site.

Two Victorian homes anchor opposite ends of the manicured grounds that also include citrus groves and a rose garden and gazebo that are popular for weddings. One of the homes, the Kellogg House, is completely restored and open for tours. The Maag House is under restoration and will be open by 2010.

The Kellogg House was built by Hiram Clay Kellogg, who also happened to be of the first civil engineers to work on taming the Santa Ana River. He oversaw the development of irrigation diversions for the Santa Ana Valley Irrigation Company, and in 1906, he became head of the Newport Protection District, which managed flood-protection efforts on the lower river. His son, H. Clay Kellogg II, founded the Kellogg Supply Company, which collected sludge from the bottom of the Santa Ana River, composted it, and then sold it back to farmers to supplement their agricultural soils.

# Diego Sepulveda Adobe
# (Historical Marker #227)

**ACCESS:** 1900 Adams Ave., Costa Mesa, 949-631-5918. Open the first and third Saturday of every month, from noon to 4 PM or by appointment.

Built between 1817 and 1823, the Diego Sepulveda Adobe has gone from modest earthen structure to elaborate ranch house and back. Today, it serves as a museum showcasing all of the eras for which it served.

Built as an outpost of the Mission San Juan Capistrano to watch over cattle and Indians, the small building was originally little more than four walls and a thatched roof. Resting on a bluff above the Santa Ana River in modern-day Costa Mesa, the adobe would have looked down on the Native American village of "Lukup," as well as thousands of acres of grazing land. From the bluff-top view, residents of the adobe also would have been able to spot ships along the coast. The location was so important that in 1827, the friars at Mission San Juan Capistrano considered moving their entire operation to this location.

With the partitioning of mission lands a few years later, the estancia became property of Diego Sepulveda, who owned much of the riverside lands in Orange County. Sometime around 1890, Gabe Allen, a Mexican War veteran, acquired the adobe from Sepulveda. In 1939, the Adams family, for which the nearby road is named, acquired the home. It has since served as an American Legion Post and once was owned by the well-known bean-growing family, the Segerstroms. It was donated to the city in 1963 and has been part of Estancia Park since that time.

# THE FUTURE OF THE SANTA ANA RIVER: FREE FLOWING OR FREEWAY?

For centuries, the Santa Ana River has irrigated the crops, quenched the thirst of a rapidly growing population, and provided relief from an evermore concrete civilization. It is a place where trees grow tall, birds sing loud, and people can, for at least a moment, forget the stress of their urban surroundings. But for how much longer can the river provide this increasingly important service?

The population of the watershed has grown tremendously in the last century, reaching nearly 5 million people by 2005. The Santa Ana River watershed consistently ranks as one of the fastest-growing regions in the country. Its economy would rank in the world's top 15 if it were an independent country. And with all of this growth, we continue to count on the Santa Ana River for more.

At the same time that we humans extract more resources, alter more natural processes, and force the river to convey flood waters through a more confined setting, the river must also continue serving the nonhuman inhabitants of the watershed. It is home to two dozen rare, threatened, and endangered species and serves as an important stop for birds migrating birds up and down the Pacific Flyway.

Developers and urban planners too often see the river as a liability more than a resource. Buildings are designed with their backs to the river rather than embracing it as part of the design. In some communities, the river has been a dividing line rather than a connection.

*left:* **The head of Santa Ana Canyon**

With the initiation of the Santa Ana River Mainstem Project in full swing by the 1990s, the future of the river seemed doomed to follow its cousin to the north, the Los Angeles River, to a slow, industrial demise that has taken supporters of that river decades to begin to overcome.

Even after the completion of two major dams and the concrete channeling of the river's lower reaches, efforts to further entomb the Santa Ana River press on. Some would like to see a freeway elevated above the river, or, worse yet, a cap placed over it to create the world's largest boxed culvert. Proponents of the project say extending the 57 Freeway down the river would ease traffic congestion on other clogged arteries and connect Inland Empire and eastern Los Angeles County residents to South Coast Plaza and the Costa Mesa financial district.

Others want more concrete upstream to increase future development potential. Political decisions have stripped critical habitat designations from much of the river's path, making development around and within the river easier and more likely.

Like a rebel army, often disorganized and under funded, a small band of river rats and watershed heroes have emerged to preserve, protect, and restore the Santa Ana River and its natural and recreational resources. They can be found on Saturdays up and down the river donning binoculars, rakes, shovels, and garbage bags. Some carry surveys or petitions, others paintbrushes to cover graffiti. They show up at city council and county supervisor's meetings to speak on behalf of the voiceless river.

Some have begun general cleanups to remove trash and debris from illegal dumpsites. Others are removing invasive plants to open the river up and create a more free-flowing, natural waterway. Still others are battling on behalf of the river in courts and political arenas. Some focus on trails and recreational resources while others tackle habitat and endangered species issues. Still others are concerned about water quality and pollution.

This final section is about these efforts, and how you, the reader, can join in the Santa Ana River renaissance and help turn this spectacular waterway into a 100-mile stretch of wild, scenic, and dynamic beauty. Some of the groups are highlighted to give examples of unique and successful projects, programs, and events occurring along the river.

Unfortunately, like so many aspects of the Santa Ana River, to include detailed descriptions on every organization would require another book. I have attempted to provide a watershed-wide overview of some of the more unique, historically important or cutting-edge groups and projects here. Contact information for dozens of other nonprofit organizations, government agencies, and special districts is also provided.

Not all of the efforts to protect or enhance the Santa Ana River occur outside the halls of government. A few politicians at different levels have begun standing up for the river, even when the efforts seem to go against the currents of political flow. Lou Correa, Orange County supervisor, former assemblyman, and, at the time of this writing, state senate candidate, has taken a strong interest in the Santa Ana River. While representing the 69th Assembly District, he authored a bill to create a Santa Ana River Conservancy. The bill would have established a governing board and brought millions of dollars to the watershed for park and recreational resource development and habitat restoration. As Correa describes it, he "was tackled at the 1-yard line with no time left on the clock." Though the bill stalled, the proverbial snowball was already rolling downhill.

As a county supervisor, Correa has continued his commitment to the watershed, vowing to stop extension of the 57 Freeway down the river. He sits on the 18-member Orange County Transportation Authority Board of Directors and has voted against the plan several times. Unfortunately, Correa, as well as Santa Ana Mayor Miguel Pulido and Huntington Beach Councilwoman Cathy Green, who joined him in opposition to the planning, were out-voted, and a feasibility study was approved. Correa and others continue to lobby the public whenever the opportunity arises.

Though the Santa Ana River Conservancy failed to materialize, it did inspire action. One person influenced by the effort was Riverside Mayor Ronald Loveridge. The city of Riverside is named for its proximity to the river and Loveridge recognized the importance of the waterway to the quality of life of those living in his city. In 2003, he created the first Santa Ana River Blue Ribbon Task Force, a 25-member group established to develop a vision for the river within the city limits of Riverside. During several meetings over a one-year period, the task force, whose members represented various public agencies, nonprofit groups, and city residents, developed an outline for the river and its related open space. The final report, "The Santa Ana River: A Vision for the 21st Century," outlines some initial steps in protecting and enhancing the river and its environs, while also setting long-term standards and goals. The Blue Ribbon Task Force was a success and the idea took off. The Wildlands Conservancy was so impressed with the idea that they began offering small grants to other cities to establish their own river task forces—and many have done so.

In a bold expansion of the concept, Anaheim Mayor Curt Pringle and his city have developed an economic stimulus plan for the river that includes new parks, trails, and entertainment development along the river through Anaheim. The plan carries the Disney Resort atmosphere east to the river and will convert the Burris Pit, a former gravel mine that serves as a groundwater-recharge pond, into the Anaheim Coves, a new environmental and entertainment area. Pringle's vision will create new trails through habitat as well as riverside dining along a boardwalk. New residential developments already have begun to spring up along the river in what the mayor refers to as the "Emerald Triangle," a redevelopment zone bordered by the river.

The fact remains, however, that none of this would be possible without the passion, dedication, and undying commitment of the community. The river would have been lost had it not been for the persistent eyes of community members and the non-government organizations they formed.

During the past century of efforts to preserve the river, one organization stands alone as the grandmother of river defenders—the Tri-County Conservation League (TCCL). TCCL has been at the frontlines of the efforts to preserve and protect the Santa Ana River for 50 years. The group was founded in 1963 by residents of Riverside and Norco to fight development of sand and gravel mines along the river in their communities. These original efforts were successful, and the group quickly grew to include members from all three counties along the river's path. TCCL officially incorporated in 1965.

Today, TCCL remains at the forefront of efforts to protect the Santa Ana River watershed. The organization works to educate and involve the community in river-related activities. One source of information is through publication and distribution of various pamphlets and booklets on particular characteristics of river. Their most recent effort is a complete list of the river's flora; however, they have also published pieces on cultural history and wildlife.

Though some of their recent efforts have been low key, the group does not shy away from a fight when it is justified. The TCCL has joined with other groups such as the Center for Biological Diversity and the Endangered Habitats League to protect various species and their habitat throughout the Santa Ana River watershed.

TCCL is a membership organization that holds at least one general membership meeting a year—usually the first Saturday in January. Members receive a quarterly newsletter, which is sometimes sent more often if issues warrant it. The group offers regular outings to connect people to the places they are working to protect, and these outings are open to the public for a small fee but are free to TCCL members.

One of the new groups on the river is the Santa Ana Watershed Association (SAWA), founded in 1996 to "promote a healthy Santa Ana watershed for wildlife and people." This nonprofit brings the strength and political power of the Orange County Water District and other supporting agencies together with the get-things-done philosophy of several resource conservation districts. This partnership to restore the watershed's ecological function has removed hundreds of acres of invasive plants and provided thousands of native replacements.

According to founder and board member Dick Zembal, removing *Arundo donax* from the river's path does more to improve conditions than many traditional restoration efforts. "Once an area is opened up, the willows and other native species return on their own," he adds. SAWA maintains a strict biological-monitoring program to prove that their efforts are working. Based on increases in endangered species populations within their project areas, they are successful.

The group, which includes many volunteers, has focused much of its attention on major tributaries to the Santa Ana River, such as San Timoteo and Santiago creeks. These tributary watersheds have been nearly wiped clean of *Arundo donax* through a methodical eradication effort that starts in the headwaters and, like the creeks themselves, works downstream. In just a few years, San Timoteo Creek has been transformed form a nearly pure stand of *Arundo*, where the creek was hidden, to an open, willow-lined stream with a clean, braided flow. The creek now moves flood flows more efficiently while at the same time providing high-quality riparian habitat.

Taking the coalition theme a step further, the Santa Ana River Watershed Alliance (SARWA) has opened the doors to any group or individual that supports the goals of the alliance and signs a declaration to that extent. The goals are simple ones and include creating or updating the Santa Ana River Watershed Plan, decreasing water consumption, and increasing wildlife habitat along the Santa Ana River.

Founded in 2004 as a project of the Earth Resources Foundation, SARWA quickly grew to develop a life of its own. Established with a grant from the California Department of Conservation to reduce the watershed's reliance on imported San Francisco Bay Delta water, the alliance set out with a water-conservation emphasis, but opened the floodgates to the many issues facing the Santa Ana River today.

Now SARWA meets monthly, exploring at least one issue at each meeting. The discussion starts with a formal presentation and then goes free form, ranging from state-of-the-art irrigation practices to sediment transport around dams. Issues are not solved at the meetings; instead, the idea is to bring them to the center and provide members with the latest information that can help groups and individuals working throughout the watershed implement the best practices available.

The alliance also sponsors quarterly workshops, symposiums, and "visioning exercises," in which the community is invited to share their ideas on what they think the future of the river should be. Sometimes this includes marking up a map, drawing pictures, or just sticking notes with wishes and desires on a big board. This information is then compiled, categorized, and worked into the planning efforts of SARWA. Their big event is the River of Life Conference, which brings together 200 or more river enthusiasts from throughout the watershed and as far away as Northern California to discuss current issues and practices and to share the latest information and technology. The one-day conference is held in May to celebrate National Watershed Month and is followed by a day of tours, volunteer restoration projects, hikes, and river cleanups.

SARWA is unique because members sign on to support the goals and objectives of the alliance; just like taking an oath or signing a pledge of allegiance, this formal membership process gives strength to the organization and a clear direction to its membership. According to Stephanie Barger, founder of Earth Resources Foundation and co-coordinator for SARWA, "it's this unique structure that makes the alliance attractive to its members and effective in protecting and enhancing the watershed." SARWA meets the second Thursday of every month in Santa Ana and meetings are open to the public (for more information, see page 239).

When it comes to volunteers, few groups field more than Trails 4 All, and none works harder. Primarily interested in trail projects, Trails 4 All inadvertently got into the watershed cleanup business in 1996. After participating in a beach cleanup, founder and executive director Jim Meyers thought, why not clean up the creeks and rivers we ride, hike, and bike along, thus preventing much of the trash and debris from reaching the beach?

The first year of what has become known as Inner Coastal and Watershed Cleanup Day (takes place on the same day as Coastal Cleanup Day, the third Saturday in September.) Trails 4 All sponsored five projects throughout Orange County and hosted several hundred volunteers. By 2006, the group was hosting nearly 3000 volunteers at more than 25 sites in three counties.

In addition to the cleanups, the group still manages to focus on its heart-and-soul projects—building, repairing, and enhancing trails. The group works closely with land managers to fill in where limited budgets fall short. Ask any Orange County park ranger how much trail they can fix in a year and the answer is likely none. Ask how much gets repaired, and the answer might surprise you; volunteers from Trails 4 All often repair, reroute, and improve miles of trails through Orange County's wilderness areas. Trails 4 All also works closely with local cities like Santa Ana to build and improve trails through urban parks.

Many of the experiences you can have on the Santa Ana River were made possible by nonprofit organizations, and no other organization has done more to elevate the Santa Ana River than has the Wildlands Conservancy (TWC). There would not be a "Santa Ana River renaissance" today were it not for the efforts of TWC. In fact, they coined the phrase.

Through their funding efforts, there are trails today where just a few years ago there was none. There are parks where once there were just vacant lots. There are restrooms, nature centers, and interpretive programs where just a few years ago none was available. There are elected officials thinking about and acting on behalf of the river, where, in the recent past, few were willing or interested.

The Wildlands Conservancy is what you could expect to get if you gave John Muir the capital resources of a bank. They are the Nature Conservancy without the corporate baggage. Unlike John Muir's Sierra Club or the Nature Conservancy, the Wildlands Conservancy believes that to protect our natural resources and wild places, we must focus on our urban communities and the thousands of young people who live in them. To this end, the Wildlands Conservancy operates from a two-part mission: To preserve the beauty and biodiversity of the earth, and to fund programs so that every child may know the wonder and joy of nature. TWC has protected more than three-quarters of a million acres of Southern California land, supported the ecological restoration of even more, and provided the financial support so that underserved communities get the opportunity to experience these places.

When important properties come onto the market, the conservancy often works to secure their purchase. Once they purchase it, TWC turns the land over to an appropriate manager. Examples of this partnership along the Santa Ana River include Colton Regional Park and Chino Hills State Park. Sometimes, the conservancy holds onto the land and manages it to best serve their mission. The Wildlands Conservancy has also funded many other projects along the river that did not include land acquisition, such as the expansion of the Hidden Valley Wildlife Area Nature Center and the funding of trail connections throughout Riverside County.

In addition to supporting individual projects and programs, TWC is instrumental in bringing together the various parties working on the river. They do this through working groups that meet regularly, and they also sponsor the annual Santa Ana River Symposium, where the many parties interested in the river come together to present their progress and share their dreams. The symposia usually are held in spring at a venue along the river, and they focus on the many aspects of the river renaissance, from recreation and urban blight to restoration and historic preservation. TWC also has added 500,000 acres to Joshua Tree and Death Valley national parks and the Mojave Desert Preserve, and the group owns and manages the largest private nature reserve on the West Coast, the 95,000-acre Wind Wolves Preserve in the San Emigdio Mountains and San Joaquin Valley.

The Wildlands Conservancy is responsible for encouraging the many cities along the river to follow Riverside's lead and form a blue ribbon committee or task force to study and set a vision for the river in their jurisdiction. At the time of this writing, more than a half dozen of the 17 cities that border the river have initiated the visioning projects. When all the cities along the river have completed their studies, a master plan for the river essentially will have been written.

Although Lou Correa's efforts to establish a Santa Ana River Conservancy failed, the Santa Ana River task forces sponsored by the Wildlands Conservancy may achieve Correa's ultimate goal—bringing much-needed resources to the watershed. Imagine the political power of a plan developed and supported by three counties and 17 cities. This goal is real, and with the guidance of the Wildlands Conservancy, it will be achieved.

Now you, the reader, know some of the players and history of the river. In the following pages are more contacts. So take this information, get involved, get your feet wet in the rejuvenating waters of the Santa Ana River, and participate in its renaissance.

# TRIPS BY THEME

## Family Trips

## Bicycle Trips

## Wilderness Trips

## Equestrian Trips

## Boat/Kayak/Canoe Trips

Baldwin Lake Ecological Reserve (page 59)
Big Bear Discovery Center (page 63)
Fairmount Park (page 88)
Prado Basin Recreation Area (page 103)
Santa Ana River Mouth and Least Tern Reserve (page 104)
Upper Newport Bay (page 148)
Lake Hemet (page 178)
Irvine Lake (page 189)


## Interpretive Center/Museum Trips

Big Bear Discovery Center (page 63)
Barton Flats Visitor Center (page 70)
Colton Regional Park (page 83)
Rancho Jurupa Regional Park (page 95)
Louis Robidoux Nature Center (page 97)
Hidden Valley Wildlife Area (page 99)
Prado Dam Visitors Center (page 106)
Chino Hills State Park (page 112)
Fairview Park (page 139)
Bolsa Chica Ecological Reserve (page 146)
Upper Newport Bay (page 148)
Mt. San Jacinto State Park (page 176)
Tucker Wildlife Sanctuary (page 186)
Irvine Regional Park (page 190)
Santiago Park Nature Reserve (page 199)
Asistencia (page 208)
Agua Mansa Cemetery (page 209)
Jensen-Alvarado Ranch Historic Park and Museum (page 210)
Yorba-Slaughter Adobe (page 212)
Susan Bixby Bryant House and Garden (page 214)
Centennial Heritage Museum (page 217)
Diego Sepulveda Adobe (Historical Marker #227) (page 219)

## Camping Trips

# IMPORTANT RESOURCES

## Government Agencies

### Federal

US Army Corps of Engineers
Los Angeles District
PO Box 2711
Los Angeles, California 90053
213-452-3961
www.spl.usace.army.mil

US Fish and Wildlife Service
6010 Hidden Valley Road
Carlsbad, California 92011
760-431-9440
www.fws.gov

US Forest Service
602 Tippecanoe Ave.
San Bernardino, CA 92408
909-382-2600
www.fs.fed.us/r5/sanbernardino
or www.bigbeardiscoverycenter.com

### State

California Department of Fish
    and Game
Region 5 (Orange County)
4949 Viewridge Ave.
San Diego, California 92123
858-467-4201
www.dfg.ca.gov

California Department of Parks
    and Recreation
Inland Empire District
17801 Lake Perris Drive
Perris, California 92571
951-443-2423
www.parks.ca.gov

Region 6 (Riverside and
    San Bernardino Counties)
3602 Inland Empire Blvd.
Ontario, California 91764
909-484-0167 or 562-430-7212
www.dfg.ca.gov

State Water Resources Control Board
(Santa Ana Regional)
3737 Main Street, Suite 500
Riverside, California 92501
951-782-4130
www.swrcb.ca.gov

## County

Orange County Flood Control District
PO Box 4048
Santa Ana, California 92702
300 North Flower Street, 7th Floor
Santa Ana, California 92703
714-834-5618
www.ocflood.com

Orange County Harbors, Beaches,
and Parks
1 Irvine Park Road
Orange, California 92869
714-973-6865
www.ocparks.com

Riverside County Flood Control
and Water Conservation District
1995 Market Street
Riverside, California 92501
951-955-1200
www.floodcontrol.co.riverside.ca.us

Riverside County Regional Parks
and Open-Space District
4600 Crestmore Road
Riverside, California 92509
951-955-4310
www.riversidecountyparks.org

San Bernardino County
Flood Control District
825 East Third Street
San Bernardino, California 92415
909-387-7906
www.sb.county.gov

San Bernardino County Parks
777 East Rialto Ave.
San Bernardino, California 92415
909-387-2757
www.sb.county.gov

## Special Districts

Big Bear Municipal Water District
PO Box 2863/40524 Lakeview Drive
Big Bear Lake, California 92315
909-866-5796
www.bbmwd.org

Eastern Municipal Water District
2270 Trumble Road
PO Box 8300
Perris, California 92572
951-928-3777
www.emwd.com

Inland Empire Utilities District
6075 Kimball Ave.
Chino, California 91710
909-993-1600
www.ieua.org

Orange County Sanitation District
10844 Ellis Ave.
Fountain Valley, California 92708
714-962-2411
www.ocsd.com

Orange County Transportation
Authority
550 South Main Street
PO Box 14184
Orange, California 92863
714-636-7433
www.octa.net

Orange County Water District
PO Box 8300
Fountain Valley, California 92728
10500 Ellis Ave.
Fountain Valley, California 92708
714-378-3200
www.ocwd.com

Riverside Transit Authority
1825 Third Street
Riverside, California 92517
951-565-5000
www.riversidetransit.com

**Special Districts** *(continued)*

San Bernardino Valley Municipal
  Water District
1350 South E Street
San Bernardino, California 92408
909-387-9200
www.sbvmwd.com

Santa Ana Watershed
  Project Authority
11615 Sterling Ave.
Riverside, California 92503
951-354-4220
www.sawpa.com

Western Municipal Water District
450 Allesandro Blvd.
Riverside, California 92508
951-789-5000
www.wmwd.com

## City and Other Local Agencies

Anaheim
200 South Anaheim Blvd.
Anaheim, California 92805
714-765-5247
www.anaheim.net

Big Bear
PO Box 10000
Big Bear, California 92315
909-866-5831
www.citybigbearlake.com

Chino
13220 Central Ave.
Chino, California 91710
909-627-7577
www.cityofchino.org

Colton
650 North La Cadena Drive
Colton, California 92324
909-370-5099
www.ci.colton.ca.us

Corona
400 South Vincenta Ave.
Corona, California 92882
951-736-2201
www.discovercorona.com

Costa Mesa
PO Box 1200
Costa Mesa, California 92628
714-754-5328
www.ci.costa-mesa.ca.us

Fountain Valley
10200 Slater Ave.
Fountain Valley, California 92708
714-593-4445
www.fountainvalley.org

Huntington Beach
2000 Main Street
Huntington Beach, California 92648
714-536-5553
www.surfcity.hb.org

Newport Beach
3300 Newport Blvd.
Newport Beach, California 92663
949-644-3309
www.city.newport-beach.ca.us

Norco
2870 Clark Ave.
Norco, California 92860
951-735-3900
www.norco.ca.us

Orange
300 East Chapman Ave.
Orange, California 92860
714-744-2200
www.cityoforange.org

Redlands
PO Box 3005
Redlands, California 92373
909-798-7533

Riverside
3780 Market Street
Riverside, California 92501
951-826-5808
www.riversideca.gov

San Bernardino
300 North D Street
San Bernardino, California 92418
909-384-5188

Santa Ana
20 Civic Center Plaza
Santa Ana, California 92701
714-647-5200
www.ci.santa-ana.ca.us

Yorba Linda
4845 Casa Loma Ave.
Yorba Linda, California 92885
714-961-7100
www.ci.yorba-linda.ca.us

# Nonprofit Organizations

Amigos de Bolsa Chica
16531 Bolsa Chica Street, Suite 312
Huntington Beach, California 92649
714-840-1575
www.amigosbolsachica.org

Bolsa Chica Conservancy
3842 Warner Ave.
Huntington Beach, California 92649
714-846-1114
www.bolsachica.org

Bolsa Chica Land Trust
5901 Warner Ave. #103
Huntington Beach, California 92649
714-536-5919
www.surfcity-hb.org

CalTrout
870 Market Street, Suite 528
San Francisco, California 94102
415-392-8887
www.caltrout.org

Center for Biological Diversity
PO Box 710
Tucson, Arizona 85702
520-623-5252
www.biologicaldiversity.org

Earth Resources Foundation
230 East 17th Street, Suite 208
Costa Mesa, California 92627
949-645-5163
www.earthresources.org

Friends of Harbors, Beaches,
and Parks
PO Box 9256
Newport Beach, California 92658
www.fhbp.org

Friends of the River
915 20th Street
Sacramento, California 95814
916-442-3155
www.friendsoftheriver.org

Huntington Beach Wetlands
Conservancy
PO Box 5903
Huntington Beach, California 92615
714-963-2123

Inland Empire WaterKeeper
3741 Merced Drive Unit F2
Riverside, California 92503
951-689-6842
www.iewaterkeeper.org

Orange Coast River Park Foundation
PO Box 9256
Newport Beach, California 92658
www.fhbp.org

Orange County Coast Keeper
3416 Via Oporto #201
Newport Beach, California 92663
714-850-1965
www.coastkeeper.org

Redlands Conservancy
PO Box 855
Redlands, California 92373
909-793-1800

Riverside Land Conservancy
4075 Mission Inn Ave.
Riverside, California 926501
951-788-0670
www.riversidelandconservancy.org

San Gorgonio Wilderness Association
34701 Mill Creek Road
Mentone, California 92359
909-382-2906
www.sgwa.org

Santa Ana River Watershed Alliance
230 East 17th Street
Costa Mesa, California 92627
949-645-5163
www.santaanawatershed.org

Santa Ana Watershed Association
25864-K Business Center Drive
Redlands, California 92374
909-799-7407
www.iercd.org

Santiago Creek Greenway Alliance
PO Box 851
Orange, California 92866
714-997-8886
ww.santiagogreenway.org

South Coast Wildlands Project
PO Box 1102
Idyllwild, California 92549
951-659-9946
www.scwildlands.org

Surfrider Foundation
Huntington/Long Beach Chapter
PO Box 3089
Long Beach, California 90803
562-438-6994
www.surfrider.org

Surfrider Foundation
Newport Beach Chapter
PO Box 7842
Newport Beach, California 92658
949-492-8170
www.surfrider.org

Trails 4 All
13042 Old Myford Road
Irvine, California 92602
714-734-8188
www.trails4all.org

Trout Unlimited
California Office
1120 College Ave.
Santa Rosa, California 95404
707-543-5877
www.tucalifornia.org

Urban Creeks Council
1250 Addison Street #107C
Berkeley, California 94702
510-540-6669
www.urbancreeks.org

The Wildlands Conservancy
39611 Oak Glen Road #12
Oak Glen, California 92399
909-797-8507
www.wildlandsconservancy.org

# INDEX

San Antonio, Mt. *See* Baldy, Mt.

San Antonio Creek 151

San Bernardino, founding of 41

San Bernardino Mountains Reach
overview of 5, 10, 51, 55–58
trips to 59–74

San Diego Creek 148

San Gabriel Mountains 11, 16, 163, 166, 172

San Gabriel River 11, 16, 154

San Gorgonio Mountain
glaciation and 18
headwaters of Santa Ana River and 10, 16, 55, 58
summit hike 66, 155, 159

San Gorgonio Wilderness 65–66, 69, 155, 161, 207

San Jacinto, Mt. 16, 173, 176

San Jacinto fault 16

San Jacinto Ranger District, San Bernardino National Forest 177

San Jacinto River
overview of 9–10, 154, 173
trips to 176–80

San Jacinto River Park 179

San Jacinto Wilderness Area 173

San Jacinto Wildlife Area 180

San Timoteo Creek 10, 151, 225

Santa Ana, Old 39, 43, 215

Santa Ana Canyon Reach
overview of 5, 51, 54, 108–09
trips to 112–21

Santa Ana Mountains 11, 16, 181, 184–85

Santa Ana River Bikeway
in Orange Coast and the River Mouth Reach 133
in Orange County Coastal Plain Reach 123
overview of 7
in Santa Ana Canyon Reach 108–09, 112, 118

in Santa Ana River Regional Park and Lower Inland Empire Reach 98, 101
in Santa Ana River Wash and Upper Inland Empire Reach 84

Santa Ana River Interpretive Site 71

Santa Ana River Mainstem Project 46–47, 106, 123, 222

Santa Ana River Mouth and Least Tern Reserve 144–45

Santa Ana River Regional Park and Lower Inland Empire Reach
overview of 5, 51, 85
trips to 88–107

Santa Ana River Symposium 228

Santa Ana River Trail
in Orange Coast and the River Mouth Reach 133, 136, 138, 139, 141, 144
in Orange County Coastal Plain Reach 129, 184
overview of 7
in San Bernardino Mountains Reach 58, 68–69, 72, 73
in Santa Ana Canyon Reach 113, 115, 121
in Santa Ana River Regional Park and Upper Inland Empire Reach 79

Santa Ana River Wash and Upper Inland Empire Reach
overview of 5, 51, 75
trips to 78–84

Santa Ana River Watershed Alliance (SARWA) 225–26

Santa Ana River woolly star 29, 75

Santa Ana suckers 28, 101, 104

Santa Ana Watershed Association (SAWA) 225

Santa Ana winds 21, 37

Santiago Creek
flooding of 46

fossil hunting near 19–20
invasive species and 225
overview of 11, 154, 181
trips to 184–201

Santiago Creek Bike Trail 181, 196, 200

Santiago Creek Trail system 181

Santiago Oaks Regional Park 181, 192–93

Santiago Park Nature Reserve 199–200

Santiago Peak 11, 16, 181

Santiago Recharge Basins 194–95

Seaview Little League baseball 138

sedimentary rock 15, 17

Sepulveda, Jose Diego 40, 208, 219

Serra, Junipero 37, 90, 216

Serrano Mission Indians 35–36, 37, 163

Seven Oaks Camping and RV Resort 58

Seven Oaks Dam
construction of 34, 46
endangered plants and 29
San Andreas fault and 16
Santa Ana River Wash and 75, 78–79
trails near 68–69

Seven Oaks Village and Resort Cabins 72

Sheep Mountain Wilderness 166, 168

silk production 43

Silverado Canyon 154, 184

size of watershed 3, 4, 9, 151

Slaughter, Fenton 212

Smith, Jedediah 41

snakes 25–26

Snow Summit 64

South Fork Campground and Trailheads 68–69, 155, 207

South Fork Canyon 172

southern oak woodland community 26–27

southwest willow flycatchers 28, 104

# ABOUT THE AUTHOR

Patrick Mitchell is the senior naturalist with the city of Santa Ana's Parks, Recreation, and Community Services Agency. He is also a member of Orange County's Regional Recreational Trails Advisory Committee and has been an environmental activist, educator, and researcher throughout California and southwestern North America. His particular research interests are landscape history and the relationship between nature and culture, both in current and historical contexts. He has studied recreation impacts in local national forests and works to improve wilderness conditions through educational activities. He regularly leads backpacking trips into Southern California wilderness areas, often guiding inner-city youth to their first wilderness experiences. He has participated in ecological restoration activities for more than 10 years, including management of habitat restoration at Santiago Park, the city of Santa Ana's first designated nature reserve. Patrick lives in Orange with his wife and two boys, who often accompany him on trips into the natural world.